Awaken From Death

Awaken from Death

An inspiring description of the soul's journey
into the spiritual realms upon bodily death

Part I: Awaken From Death
by Emanuel Swedenborg

Part II: Swedenborg's Epic Journey
by James F. Lawrence

With an introduction by Kenneth Ring

J. Appleseed & Co.
San Francisco

Awaken From Death

Library of Congress Catalog Card Number: 90-82092

1. Death 2. Afterlife I. Title

ISBN 0-9626795-0-X

Heaven and Hell excerpts edited by James F. Lawrence from a translation from the Latin by George F. Dole

Editor: *James F. Lawrence*

Cover & book design: *DBA Design & Illustration, San Carlos*, CA

Designer: *Lorene Ray Lederer*

Text set in 11/14.5 Garamond. Accents set in Stone Sans Bold.

CONTENTS

INTRODUCTION

There are of course many paths that lead up to the summit of Emanuel Swedenborg's sweeping spiritual vision of the life beyond. In my case, I came to discover Swedenborg through my research into near-death experiences—those compelling epiphanic revelations occurring on the threshold of apparent imminent death, that appear to usher individuals into a realm of ineffable preternatural beauty where time dissolves into eternity and God's light is everywhere. Actually, even before I came to see the unmistakable parallels between the world Swedenborg had described for us more than two centuries ago and that which contemporary near-death experiences were being vaulted into as a result of some kind of near-death crisis, others had already made this connection clear. Indeed, the first, and still in many ways the best, book to be written on the near-death experience in our own time, *Life After Life*, by Raymond A. Moody, Jr. contained a section where those parallels were explicitly discussed, and highlighted Swedenborg's teachings concerning what happens at the moment of death—and afterward. For me, then, my appreciation of Swedenborg's writings has from the beginning been filtered through and indeed enhanced by my study of near-death experiences and my pondering their obvious implications both for life after and *before* death.

The book you now hold in your hands is in fact one which, by drawing from Swedenborg's best-known and enduringly popular work on this subject, *Heaven and Hell*, provides an excellent introduction to Swedenborg's vision and understanding of the life beyond. And, as one quickly learns, this rendering is not at all one that stems from theological dogma but is, rather, rooted in Swedenborg's own personal and extraordinary sojourns into the spiritual world itself. His revelations, however, do not derive from the kind of brief and inchoate glimpses that near-death experiencers have often reported to me and other NDE researchers, but from sustained and deliberate forays into this domain. As Swedenborg himself says, he was not merely told but *shown* through direct experience what the dying person encounters, both at the moment of physical death and afterward, and he was enabled to have such experiences frequently over the last third of his lifetime, a period of nearly three decades. Thus Swedenborg is hardly just a precursor to today's NDEers; he is a true seer and, as such, he had already mapped the realm that NDE research has, with its own methods, tried to adumbrate.

What is the nature of this world? Here, Swedenborg makes it plain, we enter into a domain where the "essence" of ourselves is disclosed, and where we—and others—see ourselves with razor-sharp precision for who we really are. Death changes nothing, but reveals everything about us. This is just one of the many points of correspondence between Swedenborg's teachings and the findings of NDE research, by the way, which indicates that many persons have a detailed "life review" in which they are led to see not merely how they have lived, but into the inner meaning and motivations of their actions, and their effects upon others. At death, we enter a world, in short, where our inner essence becomes "the environment" in which we find ourselves. In the end, Swedenborg says, "everyone returns after death to his own life." A person who has lived meanly, for himself, whatever the outward form of his life may have been, finds himself continuing to love that way, cut off from the light of God. On the other hand, a person who has truly lived for others and for whom the existence of the Divine is at the heart of his life, is *already* in heaven, Swedenborg avers, and continues to experience directly the Light of heaven after death and to find himself in the company of like-minded others. Either way, according to Swedenborg, everyone "is going to be an image of his affection, or his love." So it is, if we follow Swedenborg's teachings, that we are building our heaven and hell now, and living in them now, too, depending on the inner meaning of our actions in the world.

This, to me, is the great moral lesson in Swedenborg's vision of the afterlife—and it is one which once again coincides with the moral implications of NDEs: As the beloved Sufi poet Kabir has it, "what is found now is found then." Near-death experiencers emphasize the importance of being involved with the world, not withdrawing from it; of serving others and not merely just paying lip service to traditional religious pieties; of knowing, with certainty, that God exists and that there is a life after death. For them, it is their NDEs that have made plain the undeniable truth of these things. Yet Swedenborg was enabled to see all this, and so much beyond this, through his incomparable experiences in the spiritual realm. And because of his remarkable intellect and powers of expression, his writings, as excerpted in this book, contain a depth of wisdom and understanding that no modern NDEer could ever hope to match. Which is why I say the study of NDEs only leads us up to Swedenborg's world—it can scarcely begin to suggest its compass.

Yet NDE research is, I think, for contemporary students of Swedenborg an important confirmatory source of the *basis* of his insights into the afterlife. During Swedenborg's own lifetime, and certainly afterward, there were many who dismissed his supposed visions, even while acknowledging that he had exceptional psychic or clairvoyant powers. Some, of course, thought him quite mad. However, in the light of NDEs—and literally millions of persons across the globe have had these experiences—it is no longer possible to deny that Swedenborg's visions have a definite experiential foundation. Too many people have seen what Swedenborg did, if not so far, and have drawn essentially the same conclusions as he did, for it to be tenable to explain away his experiences as merely some kind of idiosyncratic fancy or morbid hallucination. It is ironic that while many world-famous figures have of course long honored Swedenborg and recognized his greatness, it is the collective testimony of millions of ordinary men and women who have described what it is like to die which is helping to bring his sobering yet inspiring vision of life after death to many new readers today.

J. Appleseed & Co. has provided a real service in compiling this volume which will now introduce you directly to some of the essential writings of Emanuel Swedenborg on life after death. May it be a spur to you to examine further the works of this spiritual genius.

—Kenneth Ring

Author of *Life at Death* and *Heading Toward Omega*

PART ONE

Awaken From Death

by Emanuel Swedenborg

PREFACE

Today's[1] churchman knows almost nothing about heaven, hell or his own life after death, even though this is all described in the Word. It has gone so far that even many people born in the church deny these things and ask in their hearts, "Has anyone come back and told us?"

To prevent so negative an attitude (which is particularly prevalent among people with much worldly wisdom) from infecting and corrupting people of simple heart and simple faith, it has been made possible for me to be right with angels and to talk with them person to person. I have also been allowed to see what heaven is like and then what hell is like. This has been going on for thirteen years, so now I may describe heaven and hell from what I have seen and heard, hoping for the enlightenment of ignorance and the dispersion of disbelief by this means. The reason for the occurrence today of such direct revelation is that this is what "the Lord's coming" means.

[1] Swedenborg penned this declaration in 1758.

To my mind the only light that has been cast on the other life is found in Swedenborg's philosophy.

Elizabeth Barrett Browning

CHAPTER ONE

Awakening From Death and Entering Eternal Life

When the body can no longer fulfill its functions in the natural world corresponding to the thoughts and affections of its spirit (which the person receives from the spiritual world), then we say that the person dies. This happens when the lung's respiratory motion and the heart's systolic motion cease.

The person, however, does not die, but is simply separated from the physical component which was serviceable in the world. The actual person is still alive.

We say that the actual person lives because the person is not a person because of the body, but because of the spirit. For the spirit does the thinking in a person, and thought together with affection constitutes the person.

We can see from this that when someone dies, it is simply crossing from one world into another. This is why "death" in the Word, in its inner meaning, refers to resurrection and to continuity of life.

The most inward communication of the spirit is with the breathing and with the motion of the heart—the spirit's thought with the breathing and the affection proper to love with the heart. So when these two motions cease in the body, there is immediately a separation. These two motions (the lungs' respiratory one and the heart's systolic one) are the actual bonds whose breaking leaves the spirit to itself. The body, lacking then the life of its spirit, grows cold and begins to decay.

The reason a person's spirit communicates most inwardly with the breathing and with the heart is that all the vital motions are dependent on these two, not just in general, but in every area.

After the separation, people's spirits stay in their bodies for awhile, but not beyond the complete stillness of the heart. This varies with the ailment that causes the person's death, for in some cases, the heart's motion continues for quite a while, and in others, not long.

The moment this motion stops, the person is awakened, but this is accomplished by the Lord alone. "Awakening" means leading a person's spirit out of the body and leading it into the spiritual world, which is usually called "resurrection."

The reason people's spirits are not separated from their body before the heart's motion has stopped, is that the heart corresponds to affection from love, which is the person's actual life because everyone gets vital heat from love. Consequently, the correspondence exists as long as the bond lasts, resulting in the presence of the spirit's life within the body.

As to the way this awakening happens, I have not simply been told—I have been shown by live experience so that I could have a thorough knowledge of how it happens.

I was brought into a condition of unconsciousness as far as my physical senses were concerned—practically, that is, into the condition of people who are dying. However, my more inward life, including thought, remained unimpaired so that I perceived and remembered the things that happened, things that do happen to people who are awakened from death.

I noticed that physical breathing was almost taken away; the more inward breathing of the spirit kept on, joined to a slight and still breathing of the body.

Next, a communication was set up between my heartbeat and the celestial kingdom (since that kingdom corresponds to the heart in a person). I even saw angels from there, some at a distance; and two of them were sitting by my head. This resulted in the removal of all my personal affections, although thought and perception continued. I was in this condition for several hours.

Then the spirits who were around me left, declaring that I was dead. There was a perceptible aromatic odor, like that of an embalmed body. For when celestial angels are present, then anything that has to do with a corpse is perceived as something aromatic, which prevents spirits from coming near when they perceive it. This is how evil spirits are kept away from a person's spirit when he is just being led into eternal life.

The angels who sat by my head were silent, only their thoughts communicating with mine. When these thoughts are accepted, the angels know that the person's spirit is in a state to be led out of his body. The communication of their thoughts was accomplished by their looking at my face, this being in fact how communication of thoughts takes place in heaven.

Since I still had thought and perception in order to know and remember how awakening happens, I did perceive that the angels first tried to discover what my thinking was, whether it was like the thinking of people who die, which is normally about eternal life. I also perceived that they wanted to keep my mind in that thinking.

Later on, I was told that a person's spirit is kept in its last thought when the body dies, until it returns to the thoughts that stemmed from the affection of its general or ruling love in the world.

Especially, I was allowed to perceive and feel that there was a pulling, a kind of a drawing of the more inward elements of my mind—hence of my spirit—out of my body. I was told that this is done by the Lord, and is the source of resurrection.

When celestial angels are with people who have been awakened, they do not leave them: for they love each and every one. But when spirits are the kind who cannot be in fellowship with celestial angels any longer, then they want to get away from them.

When this happens, angels from the Lord's spiritual kingdom come, through whom spirits are granted the benefit of light. For up to this point they have not seen anything: they have only thought.

I was shown how this happens, too. Those angels seemed in a way to roll back a covering of the left eye toward the bridge of the nose, so that the eye was opened and enabled to see. A spirit's whole perception is that this is what happens, but it only seems that way.

Once this covering seems to have been rolled back, something bright but hazy is visible, rather like what a person sees through half open eyelids when he first wakes up. At this point, the bright hazy something seemed to me to be of a heavenly color: but then I was told that this varies.

After this, I felt something being softly rolled off my face, which brought about a spiritual thought. This rolling off from the face is an appearance as well, serving to depict that the person has come from natural thought into spiritual thought. The angels take the greatest possible care to prevent the emergence of any concept from the awakened person unless it savors of love. Then they tell him that he is a spirit.

After the benefit of light has been given, the spiritual angels offer new spirits every service they could ever wish in that condition, and teach them about the things that exist in the other life, but only as they can comprehend them.

If they are not the kind who are willing to be taught, those who have been awakened crave release from the fellowship of these angels. Still it is not the angels who leave them: it is they who estrange themselves from them. The angels actually love all individuals, and want above all to be of service to them, to teach them, and to lead them into heaven. They find their highest delight in this.

When spirits have thus estranged themselves, they are taken away by good spirits, who offer them all kinds of help as long as they are in fellowship with them. But if their life in the world was of a kind to make fellowship with good spirits impossible, then they crave release from them as well. This happens as long and as often as necessary, until they join the kind of spirits who wholly fit in with their life in the world, among whom they find their kind of life. Then, remarkably, they lead the same kind of life they led in the world.

This introductory phase of people's life after death, however, lasts only a few days. In the following pages we shall describe how they are guided from one state to another, and finally into heaven or hell. This again is something I have been given to know through a good deal of experience.

I have talked with some people on the third day after their departure, at which time the events described above were completed. I have even talked with three people I had known in the world, telling them that their funeral rites were now being arranged for the burial of their bodies. I said, "for their burial." When they heard this, they were struck with astonishment, saying that they were alive: people were burying only the thing that had served them in the world.

Later, they were quite amazed that while they lived in the flesh they had not believed in this kind of life after death, especially that almost everyone in the church shared this disbelief.

People who have not believed, while in the world, in any life of the soul after the life of the body, are acutely embarrassed when they realize that they are alive. But people who have convinced themselves of this opinion make friends with others of like mind and are separated from people who were in faith. For the most part, they are attached to some hellish community, because people of this sort have denied the divine and despised the true elements of the church. In fact, to the extent that people convince themselves in opposition to the eternal life of their soul, they also convince themselves in opposition to the things that belong to heaven and the church.

It was indeed Swedenborg who affirmed for the modern world, as against the abstract reasoning of the learned, the doctrine and practice of the desolate places, of shepherds and midwives, and discovered a world of spirits where there was a scenery like that of the earth, human forms, grotesque or beautiful, senses that knew pleasure and pain, marriage and war, all that could be painted upon canvas or put into stories.

William Butler Yeats

CHAPTER TWO

A Person Leaves Nothing Behind Except an Earthly Body

Numerous experiences in the spiritual world have made it clear to me that when people cross over from the natural into the spiritual world, which happens when they die, they carry with them everything that is theirs, or everything belonging to their personhood, except their earthly body. For when people enter the spiritual world, or the life after death, they are in a similar body to their body in this world. There seems to be no difference, since they do not feel or see any difference. But their body is spiritual, and so is separated and purified from earthly elements. Further, when something spiritual touches and sees something spiritual, it is just the same as when something natural touches and sees something natural.

As a result, when people become spirits, they cannot tell that they are not in the body they had in the world, and consequently do not know that they have died.

Further, people in the spiritual world enjoy every outward and inward sense they enjoyed in this world. As before, they see; as before, they hear and speak, they smell and taste; as before they feel the pressure when they are touched. They still yearn, wish, crave, think, ponder, are moved, love, and intend as before. A person who enjoyed scholarly work reads and writes as before. In a word, when people cross from one life to the other, or from one world to the other, it is as though they had gone from one place to another and had taken with them all the things they possessed in their own right as a person. This holds true to the point that one cannot say that people lose anything of their own after death, which is a death of the earthly body alone.

They even carry their natural memory with them. For they keep all the things they have heard, seen, read, learned, or thought in the world from earliest infancy right to the last moment of their life. However, since the natural items that dwell in their memory cannot be reproduced in a spiritual world, they become inactive the way they do with a person who is not thinking about them. Still, they can be duplicated when it pleases the Lord.

We shall have more to say shortly, however, about this memory and its state after death.

Sense-oriented people are quite incapable of believing that the condition after death is like this, since they do not grasp it. For sense-oriented people can only think in terms of nature, even about spiritual matters. So if they do not sense something—that is, see it with their physical eyes and touch it with their hands—they say that it does not exist, as with the disciple Thomas (John 20:25, 27, 29).

The difference between people's life in the spiritual world and their life in the natural world, however, is substantial, both in regard to their outer senses and their affections. People who are in heaven have far more refined senses (that is, they see and hear far more precisely) and they think more wisely than when they were in the world. For they see by heaven's light, which surpasses earth's light by many degrees; they hear, too, through a spiritual atmosphere, which also surpasses the earthly one by many degrees.

The difference for these outer senses is like the difference between something clear and something veiled by a cloud in the world, or between noonday light and evening shadows. Heaven's light, being the divine-true, actually gives angels' sight the ability to notice and distinguish the tiniest things. Further, their outer sight corresponds to an inner sight or discernment. For the one sight, for angels, flows into the other so that they act as one, which is why they have such keenness. In like fashion too, their hearing corresponds to their perception, which is a matter of both discernment and intention. So they notice in a speaker's tone and words the tiniest details of his affection and thought—matters of affection in the tone, and matters of thought in the words.

For angels, though, the other senses are not so refined as the senses of sight and hearing, because sight and hearing rather than the others are the servants of their intelligence and wisdom.

If the other senses operated at a like level of refinement, they would detract from the light and pleasure of their wisdom and bring in a delight in pleasures of various cravings of the body. These veil and cripple the discernment to the extent that they assume leading roles, as happens with people in the world who are sluggish and dull in matters of spiritual truth to the extent that they gratify their taste and give in to the panderings of the sense of physical touch.

From frequent encounters with the wisdom of heaven's angels, we can conclude that the more inward senses of heaven's angels, belonging to their thought and affection, are more refined and more perfect than those they had in the world. The difference between the state of people in hell and their state in the world is also substantial. Great as is the perfection and excellence of outer and inner senses for angels who are in heaven, just as great is the imperfection for people who are in hell.

As to the retention by people from the world of their whole memory, this has been shown me by many things. I have seen and heard quite a few things worth relating, and should like to tell some of them in sequence. There were people who denied crimes and disgraceful things they had committed in the world. So lest people believe them innocent, all things were uncovered and reviewed out of their memory, in sequence, from their earliest age to the end. Foremost were matters of adultery and whoredom.

There were some people who had taken others in by evil devices and who had stolen. Their wiles and thefts were recounted one after another—many of them things hardly anyone in the world had known other than the thieves themselves. They admitted them, too (since they were made clear as daylight), together with every thought, intent, pleasure, and fear which had then combined to agitate their spirits.

There were people who took bribes and made a profit out of judicial decisions. These people were examined from their memory in similar fashion, and from this source everything they had done from the beginning to the end of their tenure of office was reviewed. There were details about how much and what kind, about the time, about the state of their mind and intent, all cast together in their remembrance, now brought out into sight, running past several hundred.

This has been done with other people, and, remarkably, their very diaries where they wrote things like this have been opened and read right in front of them, page by page.

There were people who had lured virgins into dishonor and had violated chastity, who were called to a similar judgment, with details extracted and narrated from their memory. The actual faces of the virgins and other women were produced just as though they were there, with the locales, the voices, the moods. This was just as immediate as when something is presented to the sight. Sometimes these demonstrations lasted for some hours.

There was one person who thought nothing of disparaging others. I heard his disparaging remarks repeated in their sequence, his defamations as well, in the actual words—whom they were about, whom they were addressed to. All these elements were set forth and presented together in wholly life-like fashion; yet the details had been studiously covered up by him while he had lived in the world.

There was a particular person who had robbed a relative of his inheritance by some crafty device. He too was refuted and judged in a similar way. Strange as it seems, the letters and papers which had passed between them were read in my hearing, and they said that not a word was missing. This same person, shortly before his death, had secretly killed a neighbor by poison. This was laid bare in the following way. A trench seemed to be dug at his feet, and after it was dug out, a man emerged as though from a tomb and shouted at him, "What have you done to me?" Then everything was unveiled—how the poisoner had talked with him as a friend and had offered him a drink, then what he had planned beforehand and what happened afterwards. Once these matters were uncovered, it was clear that his inner condition was attracting him to hellish states.

In short, all spirits who have embraced evil are shown clearly their evil deeds, crimes, thefts, deceits, and devices. These are brought out of their own memory and proven; there is no room left for denial, since all the attendant circumstances are visible at once.

I have even heard the things which a person thought during a month seen and reviewed by angels out of his memory, a day at a time without error—things recalled as though the person were engaged in them at the time they happened.

We can conclude from these instances that people carry with them their whole memory, and that nothing is so well hidden in the world that it is not brought out into the open after death, in public, in keeping with the Lord's words,

> Nothing is concealed that will not be uncovered. and nothing hidden that will not be recognized. So what you have said in the darkness will be heard in the light, and what you have said in the ear . . . will be proclaimed on the housetops.
>
> (Luke 12:2-3)

When people's deeds are being laid bare to them after death, the angels who are given responsibility for examining them look carefully at their faces. The examination then spreads through their whole body, beginning with the fingers of one hand, then the other, and continuing in this fashion through the whole.

Because I was puzzled as to the reason for this, it was unveiled, as follows. Just as the details of thought and intention are written on the brain because their origins are there, so they are written on the entire body as well, because all elements of thought and intention move out from their origins into the entire body, where they are bounded as being in their final forms. This is why the things that are written in a person's memory, that have come from intention and consequent thought, are not written on the brain alone, but on the whole person, where they occur in a pattern that follows the pattern of the parts of the body.

This enabled me to see that people's overall quality is the same as the quality of their intention and consequent thought, even to the point that evil people are their own "evil" and good people are their own "good."

We can also draw a conclusion from these considerations about the meaning of a person's "book of life" mentioned in the Word. It is indeed the fact that everything—both deeds and thoughts—is written on the whole person, seeming to be read in a book when called from the memory, and to be seen in visual likeness when the spirit is examined in heaven's light.

I should like to append a noteworthy occurrence that involves human memory as it endures after death, an occurrence which convinced me that it is not just the broad outlines that have entered the memory which persist, but the most minute details as well: they are never erased.

I saw some books with writing in them, like books in the world, and I was informed that these had come out of the memory of the people who had written them, without a word missing that had been in the book any one of them had written in the world. In the same way, the most minute details of everything can be drawn from people's memory, even things they themselves have forgotten in the world.

The following reason was then unveiled. The human person has an outer and an inner memory, the outer one belonging to the natural person, and the inner one belonging to the spiritual person. The details which a person has thought, intended, said, done—even what they have heard and seen—are written on their inner or spiritual memory. There is no way to destroy the things that are there because they are written at once on the spirit itself and on the members of its body, as stated above. So the spirit is formed in keeping with the thoughts and acts of its intention.

I know these things seem very strange, and on this account are almost impossible to believe; still they are true.

Let no one then believe that there is anything you have thought within yourself or done in secret that remains hidden after death. Let everyone rather believe that each and every thing will then be visible as in broad daylight.

Even though people retain possession of their outer or natural memory after death, still the simply natural elements it contains are not brought out again in the other life. Instead, it is the spiritual elements connected to the natural ones by their correspondences. Yet when these are presented to view, they seem to be in just the same form they had in the natural world. For all the things that are visible in the heavens look like things in this world, even though they are not essentially natural but spiritual. The outer or natural memory, however, as concerns such of its contents as derives from what is material, from time and space, and from other things proper to nature, does not serve the spirit in the same function it performed for it in the world. For when people in this world have thought on the basis of the outer sensory level and not at the same time on the basis of the inner or "intellectual" sensory level, they have thought naturally and not spiritually. In the other life, though, when they are a spirit in the spiritual world, they do not think naturally, but spiritually. Thinking spiritually is thinking "with discernment" or "rationally." This is why the outer or natural memory becomes dormant as far as material elements are concerned, and only those elements come into play which people have drawn out through the material elements and made rational while they were in the world.

The reason for the dormancy of the outer memory in regard to its material elements is that these cannot again be brought out. Spirits and angels, in fact, talk from the affections and consequent thoughts that belong to their minds. So things which do not square with these cannot be articulated, as we can conclude from the statements about the speech of angels in heaven and their speech with humans in the physical world.

This is why people are rational after death to the extent that they have become rational by means of language and data in this world, not to the extent that they were skillful with languages and data.

I have talked with many people who were believed to be

learned in the world because of their acquaintance with such ancient languages as Hebrew, Greek, and Latin, but who had not developed their rational ability by means of what was written in these languages. Some of them seemed as simplistic as people who had no acquaintance with these languages; some seemed stupid, although an arrogance stayed with them as though they were wiser than other people.

I have talked with some people who believed in the world that a person's wisdom depended on how much his memory had in it. These people also stuffed their memories with a mass of material, and talked almost on the basis of this alone. As a result, they did not talk on their own, but echoed others, and did not perfect any rational ability by means of their matters of memory.

Some of them were stupid, some foolish—grasping absolutely nothing true, not knowing whether it was true or not, latching on to all kinds of false things which self-styled scholars market as true. In fact, on their own they cannot see whether anything is true or not, which means they cannot see anything rationally when they listen to other people.

I have also talked with people who had done a great deal of writing in the world—in many different disciplines and who as a result had a reputation for scholarship over much of the globe. Some of them could actually think logically about matters of truth, about whether things were true or not. Some did understand that they were true while they were talking with people involved in the light of truth, but still did not want to understand. So these people habitually denied the matters of truth when they were involved in their own falsities and therefore in themselves. Some were no wiser than the illiterate masses. Each one, that is, had developed his own rational ability in his own way, by means, so to speak, of the studies he had composed and copied .

But as for people who have been opposed to the true elements of the church, who have done their thinking on the basis of matters of data, and who have convinced themselves of false propositions by this means, they have not developed their rational ability. They have developed only an ability to use logic, an ability people in the world believe to be rationality. It is, however, an ability distinct from rationality. It is a faculty of "proving" whatever one likes, of seeing false rather then true things on the basis of preconceptions and fallacies.

There is no way people like this can be "driven home" to any recognition of things true, since true things cannot be seen from false ones, though false things can be seen from true ones.

People's rational ability is like a garden with things growing in it, or like fallow ground. Their memory is the soil, their true data and their insights are the seeds. Heaven's light and warmth make them come up; without these no sprouting takes place. This latter is what happens if heaven's light (which is the divine-true) and heaven's warmth (which is divine love) are not let in. They are the only sources of rational ability.

It grieves angels very deeply that learned people for the most part give nature credit for everything and consequently close off the more inward reaches of their minds, so that they cannot see any element of what is true from the light of what is true, which is heaven's light. As a result, in the other life they lose their faculty of logical thought, to prevent them from using devices of logic to spread false understandings among simple good folk and leading them astray. They are banished to desert areas.

One particular spirit was feeling resentful because he did not remember a lot of things he had known in his physical life, feeling sorry about the pleasure he was missing, in which he had previously found the greatest possible delight. He was however told that he had lost nothing whatever, that he knew everything in detail. Further, in the world where he now was, bringing things like these out to his consciousness was not allowed. It was enough that he now had the ability to think and talk much better and more perfectly, without submerging his rational ability the way he had before in thick confusions, in material, physical things, which were useless in the kingdom he had now entered. Now, he was told, he had everything conducive to the uses of eternal life; there was no other way he could become blessed and happy. So it was ignorance to believe that in this realm intelligence died at the departure and dormancy of the material things in the memory. The situation is like this instead: to the extent that a mind can be led away from the sensory matters in the outer person or the body, it is raised to spiritual and celestial matters.

The nature of the memories is sometimes presented to view in the other life, in forms visible only there. Many things are presented to view there which otherwise, for people, issue only as concepts. The more outward memory there takes on a form like a callus; the more inward a form like the medullary substance we find in the human brain, which enables us to know what they are like.

People whose whole preoccupation in their physical life was with the memory, and who therefore have not developed their rational ability, have what looks like a hard callousness, with something like stringy tendons within it. People who have filled their memories with falsities have something that looks hairy and shaggy, because of the disorganized mass of stuff. People who have been preoccupied with memory because of a love of self and the world have something that looks stuck together and calcified. People who have wanted to plumb divine secrets by means of outward data, especially those of philosophy, unwilling to believe anything unless convinced by these means, have a memory that looks gloomy with a quality of absorbing light rays and turning them into shadows. As for deceitful and hypocritical people, their memory looks like something hard and bony, like ivory, which reflects light rays.

But as for people who have been involved in what is good from love and in true things of faith, this kind of callus is not visible in them, since their more inward memory sends light rays through into their more outward memory, which rays find their end-points in the objects of concepts of that outer memory—in, so to speak, their foundation or their soil. There they find wholly agreeable vessels. For the outer memory is the last member of a sequence, in which spiritual and celestial elements softly find their end-points and come to rest, when there are good and true elements in it.

People who are involved in love to the Lord and in caring about the neighbor have while they are living in the world an angelic intelligence with and within them, but it is hidden away in the most inward reaches of their inner memory. There is no way for this intelligence and wisdom to become manifest to them before they shed what is physical. Then the natural memory is put to sleep, and the people awakened to a more inward memory, then step by step to real angelic memory.

We may now state briefly how a rational ability is developed.

A true rational ability is made up of true, not false elements; anything made up of false elements is not rational. There are three kinds of true elements—civic, moral, and spiritual.

Civic true elements have to do with matters of legal decision and governmental forms in nations—in general with what is just and fair in this area. Moral true elements have to do with matters of an individual's personal life in relation to groups and associations, generally as concerns what is honest and upright, and particularly as concerns virtues of every kind. Spiritual true elements, though, have to do with matters of heaven and the church, in general to the good that belongs to love and the true that belongs to faith.

There are three levels of life in every individual. Their rational capacity is opened on the first level by means of civic true elements, on the second level by moral true elements, and on the third by spiritual true elements.

But it does need to be known that a rational ability is not thus formed and opened by virtue of people knowing these elements, but by virtue of their living by them. "Living by them" means loving them out of a spiritual affection; and "loving them out of a spiritual affection" is loving what is just and fair because it is just and fair, loving what is honest and upright because it is honest and upright, loving what is good and true because it is good and true. On the other hand, living by them and loving them out of a physical affection is loving them for self's sake, for the sake of reputation, prestige, and profit. So people are nonrational to the extent that they love these true elements out of a physical affection. They do not really love them; they love that self which these true elements serve the way slaves serve their master. And when true things become a corps of slaves, they do not gain entrance to people or open any level of their life, not even the first. They simply come to rest in their memory, as data in material form, and bind themselves to their love of self, which is a physical love.

We can establish on this basis how a person becomes rational—namely, on the third level by a spiritual love of the good and the true that belong to heaven and the church, on the second level by a love of what is honest and upright, and on the first level by a love of what is just and fair. Further, these latter two loves become spiritual because of a spiritual love of what is good and true, because this flows into them, binds itself to them, and so to speak forms its own countenance within them.

Spirits and angels have just as much memory as people on earth. The things they have heard, seen, thought, intended, and done stay with them; and their rational ability is constantly being developed by means of their memory, to eternity. This is why spirits and angels are perfected in intelligence and wisdom by means of their insights of what is true and good, just as earthly people are.

A substantial amount of evidence has enabled me to know that spirits and angels have memory. I have in fact seen that everything they thought and did, openly or secretly, was called out of their memories while they were with other spirits. Then too, I have seen that people who were involved in some particular true matter out of a simple, good motive, were initiated into insights and thereby into intelligence, and then were led away into heaven.

But it needs to be known that they are not initiated into insights, and thereby intelligence, beyond the level of their affection for the good and the true they engaged in the world—not beyond that level. Every spirit and angel keeps the amount and quality of affection he had in the world. This is later perfected by being filled, which continues to eternity. For there is nothing that cannot keep being filled to eternity; in fact, every particular thing can be diversified in an infinite number of ways and hence enriched by different elements, and thereby multiplied and made fruitful. There is no end of any good thing, because it comes from the Infinite.

Swedenborg's message has given color and reality and unity to my thought of the life to come; it has exalted my ideas of love, truth, and usefulness; it has been my strongest incitement to overcome my limitations.

Helen Keller

CHAPTER THREE

A Person's Quality After Death

Every Christian knows from the Word that the life of each individual stays with them after death. For it is stated in many places that people will be judged and rewarded according to their deeds and works. Further, anyone who thinks on the basis of what is good and really true cannot help seeing that a person who lives well goes to heaven and a person who lives evilly goes to hell.

However, people who are involved in what is evil are unwilling to believe that their state after death depends on their life in the world. They think rather (especially when they get sick) that heaven is granted to people out of pure mercy, no matter how they have lived, and that it depends on a faith which they separate from life.

There are many places in the Word where it is stated that people will be judged and rewarded according to their deeds and works. I should like to cite a few at this point.

> The Son of man is going to come in the glory of His Father with His angels, and then He will recompense everyone according to his works.
> (Matthew 16:27)

> Blessed are the dead, who die in the Lord . . . indeed, says the Spirit, so that they may rest from their labors; . . . their works follow them.
> (Revelation 14:13)

> I will give to each individual according to his works.
> (Revelation 2:23)

> I saw the dead, small and great, standing in front of God; and the books were opened; and the dead were judged by the things which were written in the books, according to their works; . . . the sea yielded up those who were dead within it, and death and hell yielded up those within them; and all were judged according to their works.
> (Revelation 20:12-13)

Lo, I come, . . . and My reward is with Me, that I may give to everyone according to his works.

(Revelation 22:12)

Everyone . . . who hears My words and does them, I will compare to a prudent man, . . . but everyone who hears My words . . . and does not do them, is compared to a stupid man.

(Matthew 7:24, 26)

Not all the people who say to me, "Lord, Lord" will enter the kingdom of the heavens, but rather the person who does the will of My Father who is in the heavens. Many will say to Me in that day, "Lord, Lord have we not prophesied through Your name, and through Your name cast out demons, and in Your name done many good deeds?" But I will declare to them, "I do not know you: depart from Me, you evildoers."

(Matthew 7:21-23)

Then you will begin to say, "We ate and drank with you; you taught in our streets." But He will say, "I tell you, I do not know you evildoers."

(Luke 13:25-27)

> I will reward them according to their work, and according to the deed of their hands.
>
> (Jeremiah 25:14)

> [Jehovah] whose eyes are open over all the ways of man, to give to each according to his ways, and according to the fruit of his works.
>
> (Jeremiah 32:19)

> I will come to oversee . . . his ways, and I will give him the reward of his works.
>
> (Hosea 4:9)

> Jehovah . . . deals with us in keeping with our ways and in keeping with our works.
>
> (Zechariah 1:6)

When the Lord foretells the Last Judgment, He examines nothing but works; and He states in Matthew 25:32-46 that people who have done good works will enter eternal life and people who have done evil works will enter condemnation. The same view is presented in many other passages about man's salvation and condemnation.

We can see that works and deeds are people's outward life, and that the quality of their inward life takes visible form through them.

"Deeds and works," however, does not mean deeds and works simply as they present themselves in outward form; it means also the way they are inside. We all do in fact realize that every deed and work comes out of a person's intention and thought. Unless it did come from this source, it would be movement only, of the kind produced by machines and models. So seen in its own right, a deed or work is only a result which takes its soul and life from intention and thought. Accordingly, it is intention and thought in outward form.

It follows from this that the quality of the intention and thought which produce a deed or work determines the quality of the deed or work. If the thought and intention are good, then deeds and works are good; while if the thought and intention are evil, then the deeds and works are evil, even though the two kinds may look alike in outward form.

A thousand people may behave alike—that is, face us with similar deeds, so similar that we can scarcely tell them apart by their outward form. But each particular one is different, seen in its own right, because it comes from a different intention.

Let us take behaving honestly and fairly with our fellow-citizen as an example. One person can behave honestly and fairly with another in order to seem honest and fair, for the sake of self and for personal prestige. Another may do the same for the sake of this world and for profit, a third for reward and credit, a fourth to maintain a friendship, a fifth out of fear of the law, of loss of reputation and position, a sixth to attract someone to a clique, which may well be evil, a seventh to deceive, and others for still different purposes. Yet in spite of the fact that all these people's deeds seem good (for behaving honestly and fairly with a fellow citizen is a good thing), they still fall short of good and to that extent are evil, because these things are not done from a love of honesty, but from a love of self and the world. The honest and the fair work for this love the way slaves work for their master who devalues and dismisses them when they do not work for him.

People who act out of a love for what is honest and fair, behave honestly and fairly with their fellow-citizens in ways that look the same in outward form. Some of them act on the basis of what is true in their faith, or from obedience because this is enjoined in the Word; some act on the basis of what is good in their faith, or conscience, because it is a matter of religion; some act on the basis of the goodness of loving others, because what is good for the other must be taken into account; some act on the basis of the good of love to the Lord, because the good needs to be done for its own sake. Those who are honest and just love what is honest and just because they come from the Lord and because the divine element that comes from the Lord is within them, making them divine when viewed in their actual essence.

The deeds and works of these people are inwardly good, and so they are outwardly good as well. For as already stated, the whole quality of deeds and works depends on the quality of the thought and intention they come from. Without these latter they are not deeds and works, only inanimate movements. We can conclude from these considerations what "works" and "deeds" mean in the Word.

Deeds and works, being matters of intention and thought, are matters of love and faith as well. Accordingly, their quality depends on the quality of love and faith, for it makes no difference whether you say "the love" or "the intention" of a person, no difference whether you say "the faith" or "the settled thought" of a person. If people love something, they also intend it; if they believe something, they also think it. If people love what they believe, then they intend it, and do it to the extent that they can.

Everyone is capable of knowing that love and faith are within human intention and thought, not outside them, because intention is what catches fire with love, and thought is what lights up in matters of faith. As a result, the only people who are enlightened are the ones who are capable of thinking wisely; and it is in proportion to this enlightenment that they think what is true and intend what is true—or believe what is true and love what is true, which is the same thing.

It is, however, worth knowing that intention makes the person. Thought makes the person only to the extent that it comes out of intention, with deeds or works coming out of this pair. Another way of saying the same thing is to say that love makes the person, with faith a factor only to the extent that it comes out of love, and with deeds and works coming out of this pair. It follows, then, that intention or love is the actual person. For things which come forth belong to the source from which they come; "coming forth" is being brought forth and presented in a form suitable for perception and visibility.

We may conclude from these considerations what a faith separated from love is. It is no faith at all, only information which has no spiritual life in it. In a like vein, we may conclude what a deed or work is without love. It is not a deed or work of life, but a deed or work of death. It contains something that looks like life as a result of evil love and false faith. This "something that looks like life" is what we call "spiritual death."

Beyond this, it is worth knowing that the whole person is present in one's deeds or works, and that one's intention and thought (or love and faith), which are the more inward elements, are not fulfilled until they occur in deeds or works which are one's more outward elements. These more outward elements are the "last things" in which the more inward things find their boundaries. Without boundaries, they are undefined entities which have not yet become present, and which therefore are not yet in the person.

Thinking and intending without doing when doing is possible, are like something on fire which is sealed into a container and extinguished. Or, it is like a seed sown in the sand which does not sprout, but rather dies, together with its power to reproduce. But thinking and intending and consequently doing are like something on fire that gives warmth and light in all directions. This is also like seed sown in the earth which sprouts into a tree or flower and is truly present.

Everyone is capable of knowing that intending and not doing when doing is possible, is not really intending, that loving and not doing what is good when doing is possible is not really loving. This is merely thinking that one intends and loves; that is, it is thought all by itself, which fades away and dissipates.

Love, intention, is the very soul of a deed or work. This soul forms its body in the honest and fair things which the person does. This alone is where people's spiritual body, or the body of their spirit, comes from. That is, it is formed entirely out of the things the person does out of love or intention. In short, all the elements of people and of their spirit are within their deeds or works.

This now enables us to conclude what is meant by the life which people keep after death. It is their love and consequent faith, not only potential, but in act as well. So it is their deeds and works because these hold within them all the elements of the people's love and faith.

There is a "ruling love" which a person keeps after death, and which never changes to eternity. Everyone has a considerable number of loves, but they all go back to a ruling love and make one with it—or, taken all together, compose it.

All the elements of intention that are in harmony with the ruling love are called "loves," because they are loved. Some of these loves are more inward, some more outward; there are some directly bound and some indirectly bound; some are nearer, some are farther away; there are various kinds of subordination.

Taken all together, they make up a kind of kingdom. Thus they are in fact organized within a person, even though people are completely unaware of their organization. To some extent, however, this is made known to people in the other life, for they have an outreach of thought and affection there that depends on this organization. This is an outreach into heavenly communities if the ruling love is made up of loves of heaven, but an outreach into hellish communities if the ruling love is made up of loves of hell.

The reader may see above that spirits' and angels' every thought and affection has an outreach into communities. But the things mentioned so far appeal only to the thought of a rational person. To present these matters directly to sense perception, I should like to append some observed experiences to illustrate and reinforce the following points:

First: After death, people are their love or intention.

Second: To eternity, people stay the way they are as far as their intention or ruling love is concerned.

Third: People who have a heavenly and spiritual love enter heaven; while people who have a physical and worldly love without a heavenly and spiritual one enter hell.

Fourth: People do not keep their faith if it does not come from a heavenly love.

Fifth: Love in act is what lasts; hence this is the person's life.

After death, a person is his love or intention.

This has been borne in on me by observed experience over and over again. The whole heaven is divided into communities on the basis of differences in the good that comes from love. Every single spirit who is raised into heaven and becomes an angel is taken to the community where his or her love is, and once there they are where they belong *[apud se]*, so to speak—as though they were at home, where they were born. An angel senses this, and makes close friends with others like themselves.

When they leave and go somewhere else, there is a certain constant resistance. This is the effect of their longing to return to those who are like themselves, which means to their own ruling love. This is how close friendships are formed in heaven. The same holds true in hell, where people also form friendships on the basis of loves which are opposed to heavenly ones.

We may establish that after death people are their love from the fact also that there is a removal after death, a kind of carrying away, of the elements which do not make one with their ruling love. If a people are good, then all the things that are discordant or that disagree are removed and, so to speak, carried away. In this way they are installed in their own love. The same happens with people who are evil (the difference being that true things are carried away from them, while false things are carried away from good persons), until finally all individuals become their own love. This takes place when a spirit-person is brought through into the third state described below. Once this has happened, people constantly turn their face toward their inner love, keeping it always before their eyes wherever they turn.

Spirits without exception can be led anywhere as long as they are kept in their ruling love. They are unable to resist even though they know what is happening and think that they will resist. Attempts have often been made to see whether they could act at all contrary to that love, but to no avail. Their love is like a chain or rope fastened around them so to speak, by which they can be pulled along, and which they cannot escape.

The same holds true for people in this world: their own love leads them too, and they are led by others by means of their own love. It is all the more true when they become spirits, because then they are not allowed to present the semblance of any other love, or to pretend a love that is not really theirs.

All personal association in the other life evidences the fact that people's spirits are their ruling love; for in fact, so far as anyone acts and talks in keeping with someone else's love, that person seems complete, with a fully expressive, cheerful, lively face. But so far as anyone acts and talks contrary to someone else's love, that person's face begins to change, to become hazy, and to fade from view. Eventually the whole person vanishes as though the person had never been there. I have often been amazed that this is so, since nothing like it can occur in our world; but I have been told that something like this does happen to the spirit of a person, which is no longer within another person's view when it turns away from that other.

I have been able to see that the spirit is its ruling love from another fact too, namely that in the spiritual world people grasp and claim as their own everything that fits in with their love, while casting off and disavowing everything that does not fit in. Everyone's love is like a spongy or porous tree trunk, that soaks up the kinds of fluid that foster the growth of its foliage, and repels others. It is like animals of all sorts, that recognize their foods, and seek out those that agree with their natures and avoid the ones that disagree. Every particular love wants to be nourished by what is appropriate to it—an evil love by false things, and a good love by true things.

Several times, I have been enabled to see how good, simple folk wanted to educate evil people in matters of truth and goodness, and how these latter ran away from this education; and when they reached their own kind, they grasped the false elements that suited their love with an intense pleasure. I have also been enabled to see good spirits talking with each other about true things, which the good people present listened to eagerly, while the evil ones who were also present paid no attention whatever, just as though they did not hear anything.

Paths are visible in the spiritual world. Some lead to heaven, some to hell; one to one community, one to another.

Good spirits travel only along paths that lead to heaven, to the community which is involved in the particular good that comes from their own love. They do not see paths leading in other directions. Evil spirits follow only paths that lead to hell, to the particular community there which is involved in the evil that comes from their own love. They do not see paths leading in other directions; and even if they do, they do not want to follow them.

Paths like this in the spiritual world are "real appearances" which correspond to true or false things, which is why "paths" in the Word have the same meaning.

These sample experiences reinforce the things already stated on the grounds of reason, namely that after death people are their own love and their own intention. We say "intention" because people's actual intention is their love.

To eternity, people stay the way they are as far as their ruling love or intention is concerned, which too I have had supported by a good deal of experience. I have been allowed to talk with some people who had lived two thousand years ago, people whose lives are described in histories and are therefore known. These people were found to be still the same, just like their descriptions, including the matter of the love which was the source and determining principle of their lives. There were other people who lived seventeen centuries ago, known from historical sources, some who lived four centuries ago, some three, and so on, with whom I have been enabled to talk. I discovered that the same affection still reigned within them, the only difference being that their loves' pleasures had been changed into the kinds of thing that corresponded to them.

Angels said that the ruling love's life is never to all eternity changed for anyone because everyone is their own love. So changing this for a spirit would be taking away or extinguishing their life. Further, they told me why—namely that after death people can no longer be re-formed by teaching the way they could in the world, because their lowest level, which is made up of natural insights and affections, is then stilled and is incapable of being opened because it is not spiritual. The more inward elements, which are proper to the person's mind or spirit *[animus]*, rest on this level like a house on its foundation; and this is why people stay to eternity the way their love's life was in the world.

Angels are quite amazed at the earthly human ignorance of the fact that everyone's quality is the quality of their ruling love, and at the widespread belief in the possibility of salvation by direct mercy and by faith only, regardless of the quality of life. They are also amazed at a similar ignorance of the fact the divine mercy is indirect, that it involves being led by the Lord both in this world and thereafter to eternity, that people whose lives are not involved in evil are the ones who are led out of this mercy. People do not even know that faith is an affection for what is true, which comes out of a heavenly love, which is from the Lord.

People who have a heavenly and spiritual love enter heaven; while people who have a physical and worldly love without a heavenly and spiritual one enter hell. All the people I have seen raised into heaven or cast into hell have made it possible for me to be sure of this. The people who were raised into heaven derived their life from a heavenly and spiritual love, while the people who were cast into hell derived their life from a physical and worldly love.

Heavenly love is loving what is good, honest, and fair

because it is good, honest and fair, and doing it because of that love. So they have a life of goodness, honesty, and fairness, which is a heavenly life. People who love these things for their own sake and who do or live them also love the Lord supremely, because these things come from Him. They love the neighbor as well, because these things are the neighbor whom they should love.

Physical love, in contrast, is loving what is good, honest and fair not for their own sakes but for the sake of oneself, because these are means for gaining fame, prestige, and profit. These people do not focus on the Lord and the neighbor within what is good and honest and fair, but on themselves and the world. They feel a pleasure in cheating; and any good, honest, or fair act that stems from cheating is actually evil, dishonest, and unfair—which is what they love within the acts.

Since loves do define everyone's life in this way, everyone is examined as to quality as soon as they come into the world of spirits after death, and are connected with people who are involved in a love like their own. People who are involved in a heavenly love are connected with people in heaven, and people who are involved in a physical love are connected with people in hell.

Then too, after the first and second states have been completed, these two classes are separated so that they no longer see or recognize each other. All individuals become their own love, not only in regard to the more inward elements of their mind, but even in regard to the more outward matters that are proper to their face, body, and speech; for all people become an image of their love, even in outward things.

People who are physical loves look crude, dark, black, and misshapen; while people who are heavenly loves look lively, bright, shining, and lovely. They are wholly unlike in spirit and in thought. People who are heavenly loves are also intelligent and wise; people who are physical loves are stolid and rather foolish.

When one is enabled to examine the more inward and the more outward elements of people who are involved in a heavenly love, their more inward elements look like light—in some, like a flaming light—and their more outward elements appear in a variety of lovely colors like a rainbow. But the more inward elements of people who are involved in a physical love look like something black because they are closed—in some, like a dark fire. These last are people more deeply involved in malicious deceit. Their more outward elements appear in a color that is dirty, and depressing to look at. The more inward and more outward elements of the mind and spirit *[animus]* are presented to view in the spiritual world whenever it pleases the Lord.

People who are involved in a physical love do not see anything in heaven's light. To them, heaven's light is gloom, while hell's light (which is like the light of burning embers) is like a bright light to them. In heaven's light their more inward sight is actually darkened to the point that they become insane. Consequently, they flee from that light and hide in caves or caverns, more or less deep depending on the false things within them derived from their evils. It is quite the reverse with people who are involved in a heavenly love. The more deeply or highly they enter heaven's light, the more clearly they see everything, and the more beautiful everything is. To the same extent, they perceive things that are true more intelligently and more wisely.

People who are involved in a physical love are wholly incapable of living in heaven's warmth, since heaven's warmth is heavenly love. They are however capable of living in hell's warmth, which is a love of cruelty toward other people who do not support them. The pleasures of this love are various kinds of contempt for others, of enmity, hatred, and revenge. When they are involved in these, they are involved in their own life, utterly ignorant of what its means to do something good to others on the basis of and for the sake of the good act itself—only of doing good on the basis of what is evil and for the sake of what is evil.

People who are involved in a physical love cannot breathe in heaven either. If an evil spirit is taken there, he draws each breath like someone hard pressed in a struggle. But people who are involved in a heavenly love breathe more freely and live more fully the farther into heaven they are.

We can conclude from these considerations that a heavenly and spiritual love is heaven within a person because all the elements of heaven are engraved on such a love. Further, a physical and worldly love without a heavenly and spiritual one is hell within a person, because all the elements of hell are engraved on such loves.

We can see from these conclusions that a person who has a heavenly and spiritual love enters heaven, while a person who has a physical and worldly love without a heavenly and spiritual one enters hell.

People do not not keep their faith if it does not come from a heavenly love. This has been made clear to me by so much experience that if I were to cite the things I have seen and heard on this subject, they would fill a book. This I can affirm—that there neither is nor can be any faith whatever in people who are involved in a physical and worldly love apart from a heavenly and spiritual one; there is only knowledge, or any urge to regard something as true because it is useful to their love.

Several people who claimed involvement in faith were brought to people who were involved in faith. Once real communication was granted, they perceived that they had absolutely no faith. They even admitted later that simply believing what is true and believing the Word is not faith; rather it is loving what is true out of a heavenly love, and wanting to do it from a relatively inward affection.

I have also been shown that their urge to believe was only like the light in winter. Since there is no warmth in this light, everything on earth is dormant, fettered by the cold, and lies under the snow. So the moment heaven's light rays strike the light of this opportunistic faith within them, it is not merely extinguished, it actually becomes like a thick gloom in which spirits cannot see themselves. At the same time the more inward elements are so darkened that they understand nothing at all; and these people then become insane as a result of falsities.

For this reason, everything true is taken away from people like this, things which they have known from the Word and from the church's teaching, and have said were a part of their own faith. In their place, they soak up every falsehood that is in harmony with the evil nature of their lives. All of them are consigned to their own loves, and with them to the falsehoods that are in harmony. And since true things conflict with the falsehoods of the evil nature they are involved in, they bear a hatred toward these true things and turn away from them, thus throwing them away.

Love in act is what lasts; hence this is the person's life. This follows as a logical conclusion both from the things now set forth from experience, and from the statements made about works and deeds above. Love in act is the work and the deed.

I teach a course on the near-death experience and related phenomena, and in that course I spend two lectures talking about Swedenborg's life, so that I can introduce the students to him. I talk about the fit between Swedenborg's own teachings about what happens after death with the findings of the near-death experience. I find it quite instructive. I don't know what category to put him in—sage, seer, or mystic. All of these, I think. He seems to have anticipated the findings of modern near-death experience research on the basis of his own personal experiences. It's really quite extraordinary that he could have said so much. A person who has had a near-death experience has essentially looked through a doorway. Swedenborg explored the whole house of death.

Kenneth Ring

CHAPTER FOUR

The Change of Pleasures After Death

In the last chapter, we showed that the ruling affection or dominant love in every person lasts to eternity. We need now to show that the pleasures of that affection or love are changed into things that correspond to them. By being changed "into things that correspond," we mean "into spiritual things that correspond to natural things."

We may conclude that they are changed into spiritual things from the fact that people are involved in a natural world as long as they are in their earthly bodies. Once they have left the physical body, they enter a spiritual world and put on a spiritual body.

All the pleasures people have belong to their ruling love, for people experience as pleasant only the things that they love—particularly, then, what they love above all else. It makes no difference whether you say "their ruling love" or "what they love above all."

These pleasures are of different kinds—as many overall as there are ruling loves, or therefore people, spirits, and angels; for one person's ruling love is not exactly the same as any other's. This is why there is no way for one person's face to be just like another's, since the face is an image of the person's spirit *[animus]*, and is in the spiritual world an image of an individual's ruling love.

The pleasures of individuals, taken singly, also display an infinite variety. There is no such thing as one of an individual's pleasures being exactly like, or the same as, another, whether one is following another or one happens at the same time as another. There is no such thing as one being the same as another.

Nevertheless, taken singly in people, these pleasures go back to their one love, their ruling love; in fact, they make it up, and thus make one with it. In a similar way, all pleasures overall go back to one universally ruling love—in heaven, to a love for the Lord, and in hell to a love of self.

A knowledge of correspondences is the only source of knowledge about the nature and quality of the spiritual pleasures into which an individual's natural pleasures are changed after death. In general, this teaches that no natural entity exists without something spiritual corresponding to it; it also teaches in particular the nature and quality of the "something" that corresponds.

Consequently, people who are involved in this knowledge are able to recognize and know what their state will be after death, if only they know their love and what its quality is in respect to the universally ruling love—to which all loves go back, as stated just above. But knowing one's own ruling love is impossible for people involved in love of self, since they love whatever is theirs and call evil things good, and likewise call true the favorite falsities with which they reinforce their evil qualities. Even so, if they wanted to, they could know from others who are wise, because these people see what they themselves do not. But this does not happen with people who are so entranced with self-love that they find the teaching of wise people distasteful.

People who are involved in a heavenly love do however accept instruction. They see the evil qualities into which they were born, even while they are caught up in them. They see them on the basis of truths; truths do in fact show up evil qualities.

A person can actually see what is evil and its falsity on the basis of what is true arising from what is good. But no one can see what is good and true on the basis of what is evil. This is because the falsities of evil are and correspond to darkness. So people who are involved in false things because of something evil are like blind people who do not see the things that are in the light, and they even hurry away from them like owls.

But things that are true because of what is good are and correspond to light. So people who are involved in things that are true because of what is good are sighted and open-eyed; they see things proper to light and things proper to shade.

I have been granted corroboration in these matters too through experience. The angels who are in the heavens both see and perceive the evil and false things that well up within them from time to time, likewise the evil and false things that engage spirits who are connected with the hells while in the world of spirits. The spirits themselves, however, are not able to see their own evil and false elements. They do not grasp what the good that comes from heavenly love is, what conscience is, what anything honest and fair is except for their own sakes, or what it is to be led by the Lord. They say that these things do not exist, that they are nothing.

We have mentioned these things to the end that people might examine themselves, recognizing their love from pleasures, and thereby, with enough information about correspondences, know the state of their life after death.

On the basis of a knowledge of correspondences, it is definitely possible to know how the pleasures of an individual's life are changed after death into things that correspond to them. However, inasmuch as this knowledge has not been popularized yet, I should like to put that subject in a certain amount of light with some examples from experience.

All people who are involved in evil and who have reinforced themselves in false principles in opposition to the true elements of the Christian religion, especially the ones who have cast the Word aside, run away from heaven's light. They scurry into caverns that look terribly gloomy at their mouths and into openings in the rocks, and hide themselves there. This is because they have loved false things and hated true ones. Caverns like this correspond to false things, as do holes in the rocks and darkness; while light corresponds to true things. They find their delight in living in these places, and they find living in open fields unpleasant.

People who found pleasure in secretive plotting and in working out stratagems in concealment behave in similar fashion. They are in these caverns too; and they go into rooms so dark that they cannot see each other, where they whisper into each other's ears in corners. This is what the delight of their love turns into.

As for people who have been diligent about data simply in order to sound learned, without developing a rational capacity by this means, who have derived pleasure from pride in matters of memory, they love sandy areas, choosing them over fields and cultivated lands. This is because sandy areas correspond to this kind of pursuit.

People who have been involved in a knowledge of the doctrinal forms of their own and other churches without applying them to life choose rocky places for themselves and live among piles of boulders. They avoid cultivated lands because they have a distaste for them.

Then there are people who have given nature and their own discretion credit for everything, who have used various devices to raise their prestige and to get rich. In the other life, they pursue magical arts which are misuses of divine order. They sense in these the most pleasurable life.

People who have devoted divine truths to their own loves and who have rendered them false by so doing, love things that have to do with urine, because things that have to do with urine correspond to the pleasures of this kind of love.

People who have been disgustingly greedy live in hovels and love dirty things fit for pigs, and the kinds of reeking vapors that undigested foods in the stomach give off.

As for people who have spent their lives wholly on pleasures, living in elegance and giving in to the palate and the belly, loving these as life's highest good, in the other life they love excrement and outhouses. They delight in things like this after death because their kind of pleasure is spiritual filth. They avoid places that are clean and free of filth because they find them distasteful.

People who took their pleasures in acts of adultery spend their time in brothels where everything is filthy and foul. They love this, and avoid homes where there is chastity. The moment they reach such homes, they faint. Nothing is more pleasant to them than breaking up marriages.

People who have been eager for revenge, and who have thereby put on a cruel and vicious nature, love places that are full of corpses, and are to be found in hells like that.

Other people find other circumstances.

In contrast, the life pleasures of people who in the world have lived involved in a heavenly love, change into the kinds of corresponding things that exist in heaven. These things come into being from heaven's sun and from the light that comes from it, which light presents to view such things as have divine elements hidden within them. Things which are seen from this light move the more inward reaches of angels, which belong to their minds, together with the more outward elements that belong to their bodies. And since a divine light (which is the divine-true coming forth from the Lord) flows into their minds, which have been opened by means of a heavenly love, it presents in the realm outside the kinds of thing that correspond to the pleasures of their love.

Things visible to the eye in the heavens correspond to the more inward elements of angels—to things proper to their faith and love, and consequently to their intelligence and wisdom. Since we have already begun to corroborate this proposition by examples drawn from experience, in order to shed some light on what was said above on the basis of the reasons for things, I should like to bring into consideration something about the heavenly pleasures that natural pleasures turn into for people who have lived involved in a heavenly love in the world.

People who from a more inward affection, an affection for truth itself, have loved things at once true and divine and have loved the Word, live in lofty places which look like mountains, where they are constantly in heaven's light. They do not know what the kind of darkness like night on earth is, and they also live in a climate of springtime. Before their sight, as it were, lie fields and crops and vineyards. In their houses, little things gleam as though they were made of gems; looking out their windows is like looking through pure crystal. These are their visual delights; but on a deeper level they are delights because of their correspondence with divine, heavenly things. For the true things they loved out of the Word correspond to crops, vineyards, gems, windows, and crystals.

People who have promptly applied the church's doctrinal forms drawn from the Word directly to their lives, are in the inmost heaven, and are involved in the pleasures of wisdom more than others. They see divine elements within particular objects. They do actually see the objects, but the corresponding divine elements flow into their minds instantly and fill them with a blessedness that moves all their sensations. As a result, all things before them seem to laugh and frolic and live.

As for people who have loved knowledges and have developed their rational capacity with them, who have also furnished themselves with intelligence from this source, acknowledging the divine at the same time, their pleasure in knowledges and their rational delight are in the other life turned into a spiritual delight involving insights into what is good and true. They live in gardens where they see beautifully laid out flower beds and lawns, all surrounded by rows of trees with gateways and walks. The trees and flowers alter from day to day. Their overall appearance offers pleasures to their minds, while the particular variations constantly renew them. Since these things correspond to divine elements, and since these people are engaged in a knowledge of correspondences they are always being filled with new insights, through which their spiritual rational ability is brought toward perfection. These things constitute their pleasures because gardens, flowerbeds, lawns, and trees correspond to knowledges, to insights and consequently to intelligence.

As for people who have given the divine credit for everything and have seen nature as relatively dead, simply submissive to spiritual things, and who have convinced themselves of this view, they are in a heavenly light. All the things they see before them derive a kind of translucence from that light; and within that translucence they see countless hues of light which their inner sight seems to drink directly in. They feel inward delights from this process. The furnishings one sees in their houses are diamond-like, with similar hues within them. I have been told that the walls of their houses seem to be made of something crystalline and therefore translucent, and that one can see within them something like flowing forms representative of heavenly matters, constantly changing; this because such a translucence corresponds to an understanding that has been enlightened by the Lord, with the shadows that arise from faith and love of natural things taken away. This is what these phenomena are like, and there are countless others, which people who have been in heaven describe by saying that they have seen what no eye can ever see.

They also say that, from a perception of divine elements communicated to them through these sights, they have heard what no ear can ever hear.

Then there are people who have not behaved secretively, who have rather wanted everything they were thinking to be out in the open, as far as civic life allowed. Since they have thought only what was honest and fair, based on something divine, they have radiant faces in heaven. As a result of that radiance, the details of their affections and thoughts can be seen in their faces as though they had taken form, and the people themselves, in their speech and actions, are like reflections of their affections. As a result, they are more beloved than others. When they talk, their faces become a little dim, but after they finish talking, the very things they have said are fully visible to the sight, all together in their faces. Since the things which occur around them correspond to their more inward natures. they are all in visible forms of such nature that other people perceive clearly what they portray and mean. Spirits who found pleasure in behaving secretively avoid coming anywhere near them; they seem to themselves to crawl away from them like snakes.

People who have judged acts of adultery to be unspeakable and have lived involved in a chaste love of marriage, are more in the design and form of heaven than others. Consequently, they are in a total beauty and constantly in the bloom of youth. The pleasures of their love are indescribable and grow to eternity, for all the pleasures and joys of heaven flow into that love. This is because that love comes down from the Lord's bond with heaven and the church, or broadly speaking from the bond between what is good and what is true, this bond being heaven itself, both in general and in each individual angel in specific. Their outward pleasures are of such nature that they cannot be described in human terminology.

But these things we have mentioned about the correspondences of pleasures for people involved in heavenly love are only a few.

We can know from these considerations that after death, everyone's pleasures are turned into things that correspond to them, with the same love lasting all the way to eternity. This applies, for example, to marriage love, love of what is fair, what is honest, what is good, and what is true, love of knowledges and insights, love of intelligence and wisdom, and others. The things that flow from such sources like brooks from a spring are pleasures which also endure, but are raised to a higher level when the transition is made from natural to spiritual matters.

I am as much inclined as anyone to believe in a world beyond the visible, and I have enough poetic and vital drive that even my own constricted self expands to feel a Swedenborgian spirit world.

Johann Wolfgang von Goethe

CHAPTER FIVE

The First State After Death

There are three states people pass through after their death before arriving in heaven or hell. The first state involves their more outward aspects, the second involves their more inward aspects, and the third is a state of preparation. People pass through these states in the world of spirits.

As far as the first state is concerned, the state involving people's more outward aspects, they come into this state immediately after death.

All people have more outward and more inward aspects to their spirit. A spirit's more outward aspects are the means by which it adjusts the person's body in the world (especially his face, speech, and manner) for associating with other people. But the spirit's more inward aspects are the ones which belong to the person's intention and resultant thought, which are seldom evident in the face, speech, or manner.

From infancy, people get used to displaying friendliness and kindness and sincerity, and hiding what their own intentions think. So as a matter of habit they wear a moral and civic life in outward matters, no matter what they are like inwardly.

This habit is the source of people's virtual ignorance of what lies deeper within them, and also of their inattention to these matters.

People's first state after death is like their state in the world, since at that point they are similarly involved in outward matters. They have much the same face, speech, and spirit, consequently they have much the same moral and civic life.

This is why they are then quite unaware that they are not still in the world, unless they pay attention to things that happen to them and to what they were told by angels when they were awakened—namely, that they are now spirits.

So the one life continues into the other, and death is only a crossing.

Because this is what people's spirits are like just after their life in the world, at that time they are recognized by their friends and by their acquaintances from this world. Spirits in fact perceive this not just from their faces and speech, but from the sphere of their life when they approach them as well.

Whenever individuals in the other life think about someone else, they set the person's face before themselves in their thought, together with many other things that belong to the person's life. When they do, the other person becomes present as though called and summoned.

This kind of thing happens in the spiritual world because thoughts are communicated there and because distances do not have the same attributes as they have in the natural world. This is why everyone, on first arrival in the other life, is recognized by friends, relatives, and acquaintances of one sort or another, and this is also why they talk with each other and then associate with each other along the lines of their friendships in the world.

I have often heard that people who arrived from the world were delighted to see their friends again, and that their friends were delighted in turn at their arrival. It is a frequent event for a married couple to meet and greet each other with great joy. They stay together for a longer period or shorter period depending on the degree to which they had been happy living together in the world. But unless a true marriage love binds them (this love being a bonding of minds from a heavenly love), they separate after they have been together a while.

But if the partners' minds had been in conflict and more inwardly turned away from each other, they break into open enmity and sometimes fight with each other. Nevertheless, they are not separated until they arrive at the next state, which will be described shortly.

Granting, then, that the life of new spirits is rather like their life in the natural world, and that they know nothing about the condition of their life after death, about heaven and about hell, except what they have learned from the literal meaning of the Word and sermons based on it—for these reasons, once they have gotten over their surprise at being in a body and having all the senses they had in the world, at seeing the same kinds of things, they become caught up in curiosity about what heaven and hell are like and where they are.

So they are taught by their friends about the state of eternal life, and are taken around to different places, into different companies. Some are taken to cities, to gardens and parks; most are taken to splendid places because this sort of place delights the outward nature they are involved in. Then they are intermittently led into thoughts they had during their physical life about the soul's state after death, heaven, and hell, until they resent their former utter ignorance of things like this, and resent the church's ignorance as well.

Almost all of them are eager to know whether they will get into heaven. Most of them believe that they will because they have led a moral and civic life in the world, without considering that evil and good people lead lives that are similar in outward aspects, do good works for other people in similar fashion, attend church in similar fashion, listen to sermons, and pray. They are wholly unaware that outward behavior and outward worship do not accomplish anything, but rather the inner elements from which the outward ones come.

Hardly one out of several thousand knows what inner elements are, or knows that they are where heaven and the church dwell within a person. They are even less aware that the quality of outward acts is the quality of the intentions and thoughts they come from, and of the love and faith prompting those intentions and thoughts. Even if they are taught this, they do not grasp that thinking and intending are effective, only that speaking and doing are.

Most people who are entering the other life from Christendom nowadays are like this.

These people, though, are examined as to their quality by good spirits, which is done by various means. This is because in this first state evil people say just as many true things and do just as many good works as good people. The reason for this (mentioned above) is that they have lived just as morally in outward form, being involved in civic affairs under laws, gaining a reputation for fairness and honesty, turning people's heads, and so rising in prestige and getting rich.

The prime telltale mark of evil spirits as opposed to good ones is that the evil ones listen avidly to what is being said about outward matters and pay little attention to what is being said about inward matters, which are the true and good elements of the church and heaven. They do hear such things, but without attentiveness and joy. Another distinctive characteristic is that they repeatedly head for particular areas, and when they are left to their own devices travel along paths that lead to these areas. The quality of love that is leading them can be discerned from the areas they head for and the paths they travel.

Then, too, all the spirits who arrive from the world are put into a connection either with a particular community in heaven or with a particular community in hell; but this applies only to their more inward elements. These more inward elements, however, are not visible to anyone as long as the spirits are involved in more outward matters, since outward matters cover and hide inner ones especially with people who are involved in something evil on a more inward level. Later on, when they come into the second state, these more inward elements become very obvious, because at that point their more inward reaches are opened, and their more outward ones recede.

For some people, this first state after death lasts a few days, for some a few months, for some a year. It rarely lasts more than a year for anyone. For given individuals, the difference depends on the harmony or discord of their more inward reaches with their more outward ones.

Actually, the more inward and more outward elements are going to act as one and correspond for every individual. No one in the spiritual world is allowed to think and intend one way while speaking and behaving another way. All souls are going to be an image of their affection, or their love; so in more outward things they will have the same quality they have in more inward things. For this reason, a spirit's more outward elements are uncovered and set in order first, so that they can serve as a plane corresponding to more inward things.

As the genial ocean streams imperceptibly warm and invigorates our shores, so the influence of Swedenborg's thought has for a hundred years been thawing and warming the bleak theology of the Middle Ages. His writings are today the prime influence beating down the wall of irrationality, making way for a faith that appeals at once to reason and to the heart. There is no doubt that he was one of the greatest intellects that has appeared upon the planet. . . . Swedenborg was the wisest man in millions. He was the eyeball on the front of the eighteenth century.

Edwin Markham

CHAPTER SIX

The Second State After Death

People's second state after death is called "the state of the more inward elements," because at that point they are brought into an involvement in the more inward things that belong to their mind, or their intention and thought, while the more outward things they were involved in during their first state go to sleep.

If anyone pays attention to people's lives and to what they say and do, they can recognize that there are relatively inward and outward aspects to everyone, or relatively inward and outward intentions and thoughts. This recognition is based on the following facts. If people are involved in civic life, they think about other people as they have heard about and observed them either on the basis of their reputation or on the basis of conversations with them. But they still do not talk with them in keeping with what they think, and even though the others are evil people, they still deal civilly with them. The truth of this is particularly recognizable in fakers and sycophants, who speak and act quite differently from the way they think and intend. It is also recognizable in hypocrites who talk about God, heaven, the salvation of souls, truths of the church, the good of their country, and the neighbor, as though they were speaking out of faith and love; while at heart they believe something else, and love themselves alone.

On this basis, we can establish the existence of two "thoughts," one more outward and one more inward, with people speaking out of the more outward thought, while feeling something else on the basis of the more inward thought. We can also establish that these two thoughts are separate, since people take precautions to prevent the more inward from flowing into the more outward and becoming somehow visible.

By creation, human nature is such that more inward thought acts as one with more outward thought through the agency of correspondence. Further, it does so act as one in people who are involved in what is good, since they think only what is good and say only what is good. However, the more inward thought does not act as one with the more outward thought in people who are involved in what is evil, since they think what is evil and say what is good. For these latter people, the order is inverted, with what is good on the outside and what is evil on the inside for them. This is why the evil rules over the good and subordinates it to itself like a slave, so that this serves as a means of reaching goals that belong to their love.

Because this kind of goal is inherent in any good thing

they say and do, we can see that "the good" in them is not good, but is stained by the evil, no matter how good it may look in outward form to people who have no knowledge of more inward things.

It is different for people who are involved in what is good. The order is not inverted in them; rather the good flows from their more inward thought into their more outward thought, flowing in this way into their speech and behavior.

We have mentioned these matters so that people might know that every person has a more inward thought and a more outward thought, and that they are distinct from each other. When we say "thought," we mean intention as well, because thought comes from intention. In fact, no one can think without intention. From these considerations, we can see what a "state of a person's more outward things" is, and what a "state of a person's more inward things" is.

When we say "intention and thought," "intention" means affection and love as well, and also every delight and pleasure that belongs to affection and love, since these go back to intention as their subject. For when people intend something, they love it and feel it to be delightful and pleasant. Conversely, when people love something and feel it to be delightful and pleasant, they intend it.

Further, "thought" means everything that serves to reinforce their affection or love, for thought is nothing but the form of their intention, or a means by which something people intend may come to light. This form is set up by various analytic rational processes which have their origin in the spiritual world and which are, strictly speaking, part of the people's spirit. It is necessary to know that people's whole quality is the quality of their more inward elements, and not the quality of their more outward ones apart from their more inward ones. This is because their more inward elements belong to their spirit, and people's life is the life of their spirit; in fact, this is the source of their bodies' life. Also, this is why people remain to eternity the same as the quality of their more inward elements.

Since, however, their more outward elements relate to their bodies, the body and spirit part after death; and such elements as cling to their spirits go to sleep. They serve only as a field for their more inward elements.

We can see from this just what things are truly part of a person and what things are not; for evil people, all the elements that belong to the more outward thought that gives rise to their speech and the more outward intending that gives rise to their actions are not really part of them. Those things are part of them which belong to the more inward elements of their thought and intention.

Once the first state is over (the state of relatively outward concerns treated in the preceding chapter), the people are directed into a state of their more inward concerns, or a state of their more inward intention and consequent thought—the state in which they were involved in the world when left to themselves, when their thought were free and unbridled. They slip unconsciously into this state when (as they did in the world) they pull in the thought nearest their speech, or the thought that gives rise to their speech, toward their more inward thought, and remain involved in this latter.

As a result, when people are in this state they are involved in their very selves and in their very own lives. For thinking freely from one's very own affection is a person's real life, and is the real person.

People in this state are thinking on the basis of their very own intention, which means they are thinking from their very own affection or love. At this point, their thinking makes a unity with their intention—such a unity, in fact, that they hardly seem to be thinking at all, simply intending. It is almost the same when they talk; but there is the difference that they talk with a certain fear that the things their intention is thinking might come out naked. This is because their fear became part of their intention in the world due to the demands of civic life.

Absolutely everyone is directed into this state after death because it is the actual state of the spirit. The earlier state is the way people were in their spirit when they were in company, which is not their proper state.

Several considerations enable us to conclude that this state of relatively outward concerns—the first state people are in after death, discussed in the preceding chapter—is not their proper state. For example, spirits not only think but even speak from their affection, because it is the basis of their language, as we may conclude from the matters stated and presented.

Then, too, people thought in like fashion in the world when they were "within themselves." For at that time they did not think on the basis of their physical language, they simply viewed these matters, seeing more things simultaneously, in a moment, than they could later articulate in half an hour.

Another phenomenon too enables us to see that a state of relatively outward concerns is not the proper state of people or of their spirit. When they are among company in the world, their conversation is in keeping with the laws of moral and civic life. At such times, their more inward thinking controls the more outward, the way one person controls another, to keep it from going beyond the bounds of propriety and respectability.

We can also see this from the fact that when people are thinking within themselves, they are thinking how they may talk and behave to please people and to gain friendship, good will, and gratitude. They are doing this by incidental means—differently, then, than if it were occurring out of their own actual intention.

These considerations enable us to see that the state of relatively inward concerns into which spirits are directed is their own proper state. So too it was people's own proper state when they lived in the world.

Once people are in the state proper to their more inward concerns, it is very obvious what kind of people they were intrinsically in the world. At this point, they are acting on the basis of what really belongs to them. If they were inwardly involved in something good in the world, they then behave rationally and wisely—more wisely, in fact, than they did in the world, because they are released from their ties with a body and therefore from the things that darken and, so to speak, cloud things over.

On the other hand, if they were involved in something evil in the world, they then behave senselessly and crazily—more crazily, in fact, than they did in the world, because they are in freedom and are not repressed. When they lived in the world, they were sane in outward matters because they were using them to fabricate a rational person. So once these outward matters are taken away from them, their madnesses are unveiled.

An evil person who presents the appearance of a good person in outward things is comparable to a vase, outwardly gleaming and polished, covered with a veil, with all kinds of filth hidden inside, in keeping with the Lord's statement,

> You are like whitewashed sepulchers that look attractive on the outside, but inwardly are filled with the bones of the dead, and with all uncleanness.
>
> (Matthew 23:27)

All people who have lived in the world involved in what is good, and who have acted out of conscience (these being those who have acknowledged something divine and loved divine truths, especially those who have applied them to their lives)—it seems to all such people, when they are brought into the state proper to their more inward concerns, as though they have been roused from sleep and come awake, or have come from darkness into light.

They are thinking on the basis of heaven's light, and therefore out of a deeper wisdom; they are acting on the basis of what is good and therefore out of a deeper affection. Heaven is flowing into their thoughts and affections with something more deeply blessed and pleasant that they had not known about before. For they have a communication with heaven's angels. At this time too, they recognize the Lord, and are worshipping Him out of their very life; for they are involved in their very own life when they are in the state of their more inward elements, as we have just stated. Further, they are recognizing and worshipping Him from their freedom, because their freedom is part of their deeper affection.

Then, too, they are withdrawing in this way from what is outwardly holy, and are entering what is inwardly holy, where actual, true worship takes place. This is what the state is like of people who have led a Christian life in accord with the commandments of the Word.

Utterly opposite, however, is the state of people who have lived in the world involved in what is evil, having no conscience, and therefore denying what is divine. People who live involved in what is evil deny deep within themselves what is divine, no matter how they think outwardly that they are not denying but acknowledging, because acknowledging the divine and living evilly are opposites.

In the other life, once people like this come into the state of their more inward elements, when other people hear them talk and see them behave, they seem like simpletons. For because of their evil cravings, they break out into crimes, contempt for others, acts of derision and blasphemy, of hatred, in vengefulness; they contrive plots, some so shrewd and vicious that it is almost impossible to believe that anything like this exists inside any person. At this point, they are in fact in a state free to act according to the thoughts proper to their intention because they are parted from the relatively outward factors that repressed them and held them in check in the world. In short, they have lost rationality because in the world their rational ability had not dwelt in their more inward reaches, but in their more outward ones. Yet still they seem to themselves to be wiser than other people.

Being like this, they are from time to time sent back briefly into the state of their more outward concerns while they are in this second state, sent too into their memory of what they did while they were in the state of their more inward concerns. Some of them are embarrassed then, and recognize that they were insane. Some of them are not embarrassed; some resent the fact that they are not allowed to be constantly in the state proper to their more outward concerns. But these last are shown what they would be like if they were constantly in this state, namely that they would secretly be working toward these same ends, misleading people of simple heart and faith by appearances of what is good, honest, and fair, with they themselves becoming utterly lost. For their more outward elements would eventually catch fire with the same blaze as their more inward ones, which would devour their whole life.

When spirits are in this second state, they come to look just the same as they were intrinsically in the world, and the things they had done and said privately are exposed. For since external factors are not controlling at this point, they say openly and try to do similar things without being afraid for their reputation as they were in the world. They are also then brought into many states of evils, so that they may appear to angels and good spirits as they really are.

In this way, private things are disclosed and secret things uncovered, in keeping with the Lord's words,

> Nothing . . . is covered, which will not be uncovered, or hidden, that will not be recognized. . . . What you have said in the darkness will be heard in the light, and what you have spoken in the ear in closets will be preached on the rooftops.
>
> (Luke 12:2, 3)

And elsewhere,

> I tell . . . you, for every idle word people have spoken, they will give account in the day of judgment.
>
> (Matthew 12:36)

No brief description can be given of what evil people are like in this state, since each individual is mad in accord with his own cravings, and these are all different. So I should like to cite just a few particular instances which will enable the reader to draw conclusions about the rest.

There are people who have loved themselves more than anything else, focusing on their own prestige in their duties and functions, fulfilling and enjoying useful tasks not for the sake of the tasks but for the sake of their own reputation, using them to make others think they are more important, being thus enchanted by a report of their own prestige. When these people are in the second state, they are more stupid than others, for to the extent that people love themselves, they are moved away from heaven, and to the extent that they move away from heaven they move away from wisdom.

As for people who are involved in self-love and were also artful, and who climbed to positions of prestige by their stratagems, they make friends with the worst people. They learn magical skills, which are misuses of the divine design, using them to harass and trouble everyone who does not show them respect. They concoct plots, they cherish hatreds, they are on fire with revenge, they long to vent their spleen on everyone who does not give in to them. They plunge into all these evils as far as the vicious mob supports them. Eventually, they mull over ways of climbing up to heaven, either to destroy it or to be worshipped there as gods. Their madness reaches even to this.

Then there are other types, who show different characteristics. On the basis of these few examples, we can draw our conclusions about the quality of people whose minds' more inward reaches are closed off toward heaven, as is the case with everyone who has not accepted some inflow from heaven by recognizing something divine and by a life of faith.

No one enters hell until they are engaged in their own evil and in the false things proper to evil. This is because no one there is allowed to have a divided mind, to think and say one thing while intending something else. All who are evil there will think what is false there because of their evil, and will speak out of their evil's falsity. Both their thinking and their speech will come from their intention, and therefore out of their own proper love and its delight and pleasure, in the same way they thought in the world when they were in their spirit—that is, the way they thought within themselves when they were thinking from their more inward affection.

The reason is that intention is the actual person, not thought except as it is derived from intention. Intention is a person's actual nature or bent. So being returned to one's own intention is being returned to one's own nature or bent, and to one's own life, because people put on a nature by means of their life. After death, people keep the kind of nature they have built up by their life in the world, which for evil people can no longer be corrected or changed by means of thinking or understanding what is true.

While evil spirits are in this second state, it is normal for them to be punished often and severely because they plunge into all kinds of evil. There are many kinds of punishment in the world of spirits, and there is no favoritism, whether the person was a king or a slave in the world.

Everything evil brings its own penalty with it. The two are bonded together. So the person who is involved in something evil is also involved in the penalty of the evil. Yet no one there suffers a penalty because of evil things they did in the world, but rather because of evil things they are doing currently.

Still, it comes down to the same thing whether you say they suffer penalties on account of the evil things they did in the world, or that they suffer penalties because of the evil things they are doing in the other life, because everyone returns after death to their own life, and therefore to similar evils. For people are of the same quality as they were during their physical lives.

The reason for this punishment is that fear of punishment is the only means of controlling evil things in this condition. Encouragement no longer works; neither does teaching or fear of law and reputation, because the people's behavior now stems from their nature, which cannot be controlled or broken except by means of punishments.

Good spirits, though, are not punished at all, even if they did evil things in the world, because their evils do not come back. We may also know that their evils were of a different kind or nature. They did in fact stem from a stance taken in opposition to what is true, not from any evil heart except what they had received from their parents by heredity. They were led into this heart by blind enjoyment when they were involved in outward matters separated from inward ones.

All souls arrive at the community where their spirits were in the world. In fact every person is bonded to a particular heavenly or hellish community—an evil person to a hellish one, a good person to a heavenly one. A spirit is guided there step by step, and eventually gains entrance.

When evil spirits are involved in the state of their more inward elements, they are turned by stages toward their own community. Eventually they are turned straight at it, before this state is completed. And once this state is completed, evil spirits themselves hurl themselves into the hell where there are people like themselves. Visually, this "hurling" looks like falling headlong, head down and feet up. The reason it looks like this is that the person is in an inverted order, having actually loved hellish things and spurned heavenly ones.

In the course of this second state, some evil individuals enter and leave the hells from time to time, but they do not seem to fall headlong as they do when they have been fully devastated.

While they are in the state proper to their more outward elements, they are shown the very community where they were in spirit while they were in the world. This happens in order to let them know that they were in hell even in their physical life. Still, they were not in the same state as the people in the hell itself, but in a state like that of the people who are in the world of spirits.

A separation of evil spirits from good spirits occurs in the course of this second state; for during the first state they were together. The reason is that as long as spirits are involved in their outward concerns, it is the same as it was in the world—the way evil people are together with good ones there, and good ones with an evil one. It is different when they are brought into involvement in their more inward concerns, and left to their own nature or intention.

The separation of the good from the evil happens in various ways. Broadly, it happens by taking the evil ones around to those communities they were in touch with through their good thoughts and affections during their first state. In this way, they are taken to those communities which were persuaded by their outward appearance that they [these spirits] were not evil. Normally, they are taken on an extensive circuit, and everywhere are exposed as they really are to good spirits. On seeing them, the good spirits turn away; and as they turn away, the evil spirits who are being taken around also turn their faces away from the good ones toward the region where the hellish community is which is their destination.

The greatest Swedish seer Emanuel Swedenborg has some claim to be the father of our new knowledge of supernal matters. When the first rays of the rising sun of spiritual knowledge fell upon the earth, they illuminated the greatest and highest human mind before they shed their light on lesser men. That mountain peak of mentality was this great religious reformer.

Sir Arthur Conan Doyle

CHAPTER SEVEN

The Third State After Death

The third state of a person's soul after death is a state of instruction. This state is for people who are entering heaven and becoming angels, but not for people who are entering hell, since they cannot be taught. As a result, their second state is also their third, concluding with their complete turning toward their own love, and therefore toward the hellish community that is involved in a like love.

When this has been accomplished, they intend and think from this love, and since the love is hellish, they intend nothing that is not evil and think nothing that is not false. These are their delights because they belong to their love. In consequence, they spurn anything good and true that they have adopted earlier because it was a useful tool for their love.

Good people, however, are brought through the second state into a third, a state of their preparation for heaven by means of instruction. For no one can be prepared for heaven except by means of insight into what is true and good—only, that is, by means of instruction. This is because people cannot know what is good and true on the spiritual level, or what is evil and false, unless they are taught. In the world, it is possible to know what is good and true on a civic and moral level, what is called fair and honest, because there are civil laws which teach what is false. There are also social contexts in which a person learns to live by moral laws, all of which deal with what is honest and right. But what is good and true on the spiritual level—this is not learned from the world, but from heaven.

It is possible to know some things from the Word, and from church doctrine based on the Word. But still, these knowledges cannot flow into people's lives unless in the more inward reaches of their mind they are in heaven. People are in heaven when they recognize what is divine and do what is fair and honest at the same time, behaving this way because it is commanded in the Word. This means behaving fairly and honestly for the sake of the divine, and not for self and the world as goals.

But no one can behave like this without first being taught, for example, that God exists, that heaven and hell exist, that there is a life after death, that God is to be loved above all, and the neighbor as oneself, that the contents of the Word are to be believed because the Word is divine.

Unless people realize and recognize these facts, they cannot think spiritually. Without thought about these matters, they cannot intend them; for if one does not know something, one cannot think about it, and if one does not think about it, one cannot intend it.

When a person does intend these things, then, heaven flows in; that is, the Lord's life flows into the person's life through heaven. For the divine essence flows into intention, through that into thought, and through these into life, these two being the source of a person's life.

We can see from these considerations, that there is no learning of what is good and true on the spiritual level from the world, but rather from heaven; and we can see that no one can be prepared for heaven except by being taught.

The Lord teaches people to the extent that His nature flows into their lives. For to this extent, He kindles their intention with a love of knowing what is true and enlightens their thought to know what is true. So far as this happens, the person's more inward reaches are opened, and heaven is grafted into them. Further what is divine and heavenly flows in to this extent into the honest elements of people's moral life and the fair elements of civic life within them and makes them spiritual, because—doing them for the sake of the divine—they are doing them from the divine. In fact, the honest and fair things proper to moral and civic life, which people do from this source, are themselves results of their spiritual life; and a result derives everything it is from its actuating cause, since the nature of the latter determines the nature of the former.

The work of instruction is done by angels of many communities, especially angels from the northern and southern regions because these angelic communities are involved in intelligence and wisdom stemming from insights into what is good and true.

The places where the instruction occurs are in the north, and are varied, arranged and set off according to the genera and species of their heavenly good qualities so that all individuals can be taught as befits their own intrinsic character and their ability to receive. These places are spread out on all sides, to quite a distance.

To these places, the Lord brings the good spirits who are to be taught, after their second state in the world of spirits has been completed. This, however, does not apply to everyone, because people who have been taught in the world have already been prepared there for heaven by the Lord, and are brought into heaven by another route. Some are brought in immediately after death. Some are brought in after a brief stay with good spirits, where the cruder elements of their thoughts and affections are set aside, which they drew from matters of prestige and wealth in the world, which removal purifies them. Some are desolated first, which takes place in the area under the soles of the feet called "the lower earth." Some people have harsh experiences there. They are the people who have settled themselves in false notions but have still led good lives. For settled false notions cling tenaciously; and true matters cannot be seen, and therefore cannot be accepted, until the false notions are shattered.

Teaching in the heavens differs from teaching on earth in that the insights are not consigned to memory but to life. Spirits' memories are in their lives; in fact, they accept and absorb all the elements that harmonize with their lives, and they do not accept, let alone absorb, things which do not harmonize. For spirits are affections, and are consequently in a human form that resemble their affections.

Since this is their nature, an affection for what is true for the sake of life's useful activity is continually being breathed in. The Lord does provide that individuals love the useful activities that fit their essential nature, this love being intensified by the individual's hope of becoming an angel. Now all the useful activities of heaven go back to a common use—for the sake of the Lord's kingdom, which is now their country; and all the individual, unique useful activities are effective the more closely and fully they focus on the common use. For this reason, the individual, unique useful activities—which are beyond counting—are good and heavenly. So an affection for what is true is bonded to an affection for useful activity so that the true things they learn are true things that belong to useful activity.

This is how angelic spirits are taught, and made ready for heaven.

There are different ways in which a truth suited to a use is instilled, most of them unknown in this world. Most often, these means involve portrayals of useful activities which are presented in a thousand ways in the spiritual world, with such delight and charm that they permeate the spirit, from the more inward elements belonging to the mind to the more outward elements belonging to the body, affecting in this way a person's whole being. Consequently spirits virtually become their own useful activity, so when they enter their own community, having been introduced there by teaching, they are involved in their own life when they are involved in their own useful activity.

We can conclude from these considerations that insights, which are outward truths, do not effect anyone's entrance to heaven. This is done rather by the life itself, which is a life of useful activity, imparted by means of insights.

There were some spirits who in the world had, by thinking, convinced themselves that they were going to enter heaven and be accepted in preference to others because they were learned and knew a great deal from the Word and the doctrines of various churches. So they believed that they were wise, and were the ones meant by the people described as "shining like the radiance of the firmament and like the stars." (Daniel 12:3). But they were examined to see whether their insights dwelt in their memories or in their lives.

Some were involved in a real affection for what is true, that is, for the sake of useful activities which, being distinct from physical and worldly concerns, are essentially spiritual uses. After they were taught, they were accepted into heaven. Then they were allowed to know what is radiant in heaven—the divine-true which is heaven's light there, within the useful activity which is the field that receives the rays of light and changes them into different forms of radiance.

But then there were people whose insights dwelt only in their memories, leading to the acquisition of an ability to apply logic to matters of truth and to "prove" the propositions they had accepted as principles. Even though these principles were false, they saw them as true once they had "proved" them. Now these people were not involved in heaven's light at all, and yet were involved in a faith stemming from pride (often connected with this kind of intelligence) that they were more learned than others, and that they were therefore headed for heaven, and that angels would be their servants. So in order to get them out of their senseless faith, they were pushed up into the first or utmost heaven to bring them into a particular angelic community. But while they were in the process of entering, their eyes began to dim at the inflow of heaven's light, their discernment became confused, and finally they began to gasp for breath like people who are near death. And when they felt heaven's warmth, which is heavenly love, they began to be tortured inside. Consequently they were cast back down. After that, they were taught that insights do not make an angel, but the actual life acquired by means of insights, since seen in their own right, insights are outside of heaven, while life by means of insights is inside heaven.

Once spirits have been prepared for heaven by teaching given in the places mentioned above (this takes a short time only, since the spirits are involved in spiritual concepts which take in many elements at the same time), they are dressed in angelic clothes, most of which are white, as though made of linen. So dressed, they are brought to a path that heads up toward heaven and are committed to angel guardians there. Then they are accepted by some other angels and introduced into communities, and there into many forms of happiness.

In the history of the rebellion of Man against God and against the order of Nature, Swedenborg stands out as a healer who wanted to break the seal on the sacred books and thus make the rebellion unnecessary.

Czeslaw Milosz

CHAPTER EIGHT

Leading a Heaven-Bound Life is Not as Hard as People Believe

Some people believe that it is hard to lead a heaven-bound life (which is called a spiritual life), because they have heard that a person needs to renounce the world, give up the appetites that are associated with the body and the flesh, and live like spiritual beings. They take this to mean nothing other than rejecting what is worldly—especially wealth and prestige—walking around in constant devout meditation on God, salvation, and eternal life, passing their lives in prayer and in reading the Word and devotional literature. They think that this is renouncing the world and living by the spirit instead of by the flesh.

But an abundance of experience and discussion with angels has enabled me to know that the situation is completely different from this. In fact, people who renounce the world and live by the spirit in this fashion build up a mournful life for themselves, one that is not receptive of heavenly joy; for everyone's life stays with them. On the contrary, if people are to accept heaven's life, they must by all means live in the world, involved in its functions and dealings. Then through a moral and civic life they receive a spiritual life. This is the only way a spiritual life can be formed in people, or their spirit be prepared for heaven.

For living an inward life and not an outward life at the same time, is like living in a house with no foundation, which gradually either settles or develops cracks and gaps, or totters until it collapses.

If we look at and examine a person's life with rational acuity, we discover that it is threefold: there is a spiritual life, a moral life, and a civic life; and we find these lives distinct from each other. For there are people who live a civic life but not a moral or a spiritual one. Then there are people who live both a civic life and a moral life and a spiritual as well. These last are the ones who are leading heaven's life—the others are leading the world's life separated from heaven's life.

A first conclusion we can draw from this is that a spiritual life is not separated from a natural one, or from the world's life. Rather, they are bonded together like a soul with its body, and if they become separated it is, as just mentioned, like living in a house without a foundation.

A moral and civic life is the behavioral aspect of a spiritual life, since intending well is a matter of spiritual life and acting well is a matter of moral and civic life. If this latter is separated from the former, the spiritual life is made up of nothing but thinking and talking. The intention fades into the background because it has no grounding—and yet the intention is the actual spiritual part of the person.

The considerations about to be presented will make it possible to see that it is not so hard to lead a heaven-bound life as people believe it is.

Who can't live a civic and moral life? Everyone is introduced to it from the cradle and is acquainted with it from his life in the world. Everyone, good or bad, leads it as well, for who does not want to be called honest and fair?

Almost everyone practices honesty and fairness in outward matters, even to the point of seeming honest and fair at heart, or as though they were behaving out of real honesty and fairness. Spiritual people need to live the same way—which they can do just as easily as natural people—the only difference being that spiritual people believe in what is divine, and behaves honestly and fairly not just because it is in keeping with civil and moral laws, but because it is in keeping with divine laws. For people who are thinking about divine matters while they are active are in touch with angels of heaven. To the extent that they are doing this, they are joined to them, and in this way their inner person is opened, which, seen in its own right, is the spiritual person.

When people are like this, they are adopted and led by the Lord without realizing it. Then anything honest and fair that they do as part of their moral and civic life is done from a spiritual source. Doing something honest and fair from a spiritual source is doing it out of what is genuinely honest and fair, or doing it from the heart.

The laws of spiritual life, the laws of civic life, and the laws of moral life are handed down to us in the precepts of the Ten Commandments. The laws of spiritual life are found first, the laws of civic life next, and the laws of moral life last.

People who are simply natural live by these precepts in

the same way as spiritual people do, in outward form. They worship the divine in similar fashion, go to church, listen to sermons, put on a pious face, do not kill, commit adultery, steal or bear false witness, do not cheat their fellows out of their possessions. But they do this simply for themselves and the world, for appearances.

As for people who have at heart recognized what is divine, who have focused on divine laws in the deeds of their lives, and have lived by the precepts of the Ten Commandments, things are different for them. When they are let into their inward aspects, it is like coming from darkness into light, from ignorance into wisdom, and from a mournful life into a blessed one. This is because they are involved in what is divine, and therefore in heaven.

We can now see that it is not so hard to lead a heaven-bound life as people think. When something gets in the way that people know is dishonest and unfair, something their spirit moves toward, it is simply a matter of thinking that they should not do it because it is against the divine precepts. If people get used to doing this, and by getting used to it gain a certain disposition, then little by little they are joined to heaven. As this takes place, the higher reaches of their mind are opened; and as they are opened, they see what things are dishonest and unfair; and as they see them, they can be broken off. For no evil can be broken off until after it is seen.

This is a state people can enter due to their freedom, for who cannot think this way, due to their freedom? And once this is begun, the Lord works out all good things for them, arranging things so that they not only see evil elements but dislike them, and eventually turn away from them. This is the meaning of the Lord's words,

"My yoke is easy, and my burden light."
(Matthew 11:30)

A heaven-bound life is not a life withdrawn from the world but a life involved in the world. A life of piety without a life of charity (which occurs only in this world) does not lead to heaven. Rather, it is a life of charity, a life of behaving honestly and fairly in every task, every transaction, every work, from a more inward source, hence a heavenly one. This source is present in that life when a person behaves honestly and fairly because it is in keeping with divine laws. This life is not hard.

Emanuel Swedenborg

Taller than others, this man
Walked among them, at a distance,
Now and then calling the angels
by their secret names. He would see
That which earthly eyes do not see:
The fierce geometry, the crystal
Labyrinth of God and the sordid
Milling of infernal delights.
He knew that Glory and Hell too
Are in your soul, with all their myths;
He knew, like the Greek, that the days
Of time are Eternity's mirrors.
In dry Latin he went on listing
The Unconditional Last Things.

Jorge Luis Borges

PART TWO

Swedenborg's Epic Journey

by James F. Lawrence

GENIUS AT WORK

Determining history's greatest intellect may seem an impossible task, but Stanford University decided to attempt it. Irresistible curiosity led researchers at Stanford to run a strategically designed database through the university's widely used Terman Intelligence Quotience Determinator test to see if the computer could reasonably calculate the IQs of some of history's best-known scholars. For three individuals, the program was not able to compute a precise number, saying only that their IQs were over 200. The three titans: Mill, Goethe, and Swedenborg. Interestingly enough, literary lore has it that Goethe was inspired to return to his unfinished manuscript, *Faust*, after reading Swedenborg's *Heaven and Hell*.

Up the road from Stanford at the Ripley Museum in San Francisco, another tribute is paid to the Swedish savant. Calling him the "world's greatest achiever," a lengthy resume of Swedenborg's life accomplishments is presented to visitors.

What sort of life was it that would lead the Stanford computer bank, museum researchers, and diverse thinkers such as philosopher Ralph Waldo Emerson, author Helen Keller, and writer Jorge Luis Borges to conclude that Swedenborg possessed an unparalleled genius?

A brief summary of Swedenborg's achievements is not easy to give. In the natural sciences alone, he is credited by science historians with an amazing number of significant original contributions. Swedenborg proposed an atomic theory of matter 200 years before Einstein; was first to propose a nebular theory as the origin for our solar system; was first to correctly identify the function of the cerebral cortex and the ductless glands; was first to deduce correctly that brain waves moved synchronously with the lungs, not with the heart; was a pioneer in magnetism theory; introduced the first Swedish textbooks of both algebra and calculus; wrote the most exhaustive works on metallurgy of his generation; founded the science of crystallography; designed and oversaw construction of what is still the world's largest dry dock; invented the first rational design for an airplane, for which he is honored by the Swedish Royal Aeronautical Society; invented improved versions of hearing aids, air-tight stoves, air guns, plus a design for "an underwater boat."

These are but the highlights of a science career that produced many scholarly works. Besides his passion for science, Swedenborg learned nine languages, played the cathedral organ, gained mastery in at least seven intricate crafts such as marble inlaying and lens grinding, and he personally designed and cultivated one of Stockholm's most renowned gardens.

Beyond these interests, he participated fully in civic affairs, sitting in Sweden's House of Nobles for fifty years. Historical documents reveal that he was deeply respected by colleagues on both sides of the aisle for his work on monetary and fiscal policy. He played a key role in solving a dramatic national political crisis in 1760.

With this sort of productivity, one would assume Swedenborg to be a university professor or, as a nobleman, independently wealthy and able to pursue his scholarly interests full time rather than entering into employment. But this is not the case. Swedenborg turned down the prestigious professorship of astronomy at Uppsala University, due to his conviction that Sweden most needed him in her most vital industry: mining. The Chair of Astronomy therefore went instead to Anders Celsius (the inventor of the centigrade thermometer by the same name), and Swedenborg instead devoted twenty-five years of full-time service to Sweden's industrial development.

All of this would be stupendous enough, but it cannot be fully appreciated until it is understood that these fifty-seven years of achievement were but preparatory years for what turned out to be a pivotal role in the affairs of human history.

QUEST FOR THE DIVINE

Even a casual study of Swedenborg's life quickly reveals that in his determined quest for knowledge, one consideration overrode all else: his search for the divine. Moving generally from the external physical world's laws and principles to laws and principles of an interior spiritual world, from mathematics and astronomy to human anatomy and psychology, Swedenborg pursued relentlessly an understanding of how the invisible divine animates the material. His quest had taken him throughout the cosmos and far into the mysterious depths of human beings—their physical bodies and their spiritual minds and personalities.

In the 1720s he concentrated on chemistry, mathematics and astronomy, becoming Sweden's most able astronomer. In the first half of the 1730s, Swedenborg developed an expertise in mineralogy, physics, and a general philosophy of nature. He narrowed his focus to human anatomy during the second half of that decade, while continuing philosophical speculations regarding ultimate reality.

By the early 1740s he found himself at a difficult impasse. In 1740 he produced an impressive volume on anatomy containing several insights advancing the entire field. It was hailed by scholars throughout Europe and sold out shortly, but he himself was disappointed because he had failed in his primary objective of discovering the seat of the soul. He came to the characteristic conclusion that he needed to undertake an even more exhaustive analysis and observation of human anatomy.

And so began the mammoth task of a second, far more elaborate attempt to identify and explain the actual connection between the soul and body. Laying out a seventeen-part work that would result in over a thousand pages, he was like the woman in the parable searching for a hidden coin: he was going to mount an ever-more painstaking focus until he found it. And he did find the soul, but not quite in the way that he anticipated.

THE BREAKTHROUGH

At this point he was a fifty-five year old bachelor scientist—arguably Europe's most brilliant thinker—investing the totality of his creative energy into discovering the nature of the human soul and thereby coming face to face with God. As he pressed ever deeper into contemplations on human anatomy as the home of the soul, his own inner life erupted with dreams and visions that led him into an intense personal review.

During a period from spring 1743 to Easter 1744, Swedenborg experienced a number of dreams and visions that moved him profoundly. Fortunately for us, he began keeping a dream journal, through which we are today able to understand some of his psychic process. Two personal issues repeatedly appear in his dream journal. The first came as a result of his ignoring the emotional side of his personality during his years of prodigious scientific output. As his inner spiritual eyes became more "seeing," the life of his affections came roaring to the forefront of his spiritual crisis. He had to engage the awesome energy and truthfulness of his emotions as he pressed inward. Gradually, he became comfortable with the fierce honesty of his deeper self, blending its truths into a new spiritual wisdom.

The other issue was equally central to his transformation. For a man of his abilities, it was undoubtedly a challenge to attain much humility. Intellectual pride had quietly mounted for decades and loomed as a serious obstacle to his spiritual transformation. Numerous dreams alerted him to this fundamental problem, and his horror at seeing the extent of his pride is very moving reading. It appears that a devotional intensity in giving all merit to his Creator was not only key, but seems to have been the final doorway leading to a paranormal residence in spiritual realms.

This inner and prayerful confrontation with his own soul went on for a year, finally culminating on the day after Easter in 1744 in a Christ vision of such extraordinary power that it changed Swedenborg's outer life dramatically. He put aside all activities in natural science in favor of writing and publishing a new spiritual understanding of life. The new writing he then undertook was never at odds with his basis in science, but his approach was strictly spiritual and theological.

SWEDENBORG'S UNIQUE STATE OF SPIRITUAL SENSITIVITY

After his Christ encounter, Swedenborg's inner life underwent an extraordinary paranormal transition leaving him with an idiomatic capacity for second sight unique in the annals of psychic phenomena. Any brief presentation of Swedenborg's life and journey must highlight this state of consciousness that Swedenborg maintained on a daily basis for the remaining twenty-seven years of his life. It was to enable him to produce the crowning works of his long life of achievement.

In the TIME-LIFE series of books on mysticism and spiritual phenomena, the volume on extrasensory perception leads off with an essay describing "the most famous case of clairvoyance" in history. It was in 1759, about fifteen years after Swedenborg's full introduction into his unusual access to the spiritual world. Dining along with fifteen other guests at the home of a prominent merchant in the port city of Gothenburg, Swedenborg suddenly became visibly pale and excused himself with considerable anxiety. Upon questioning, he declared that a dangerous fire had just broken out in south Stockholm and that it was spreading quickly toward his own home where his work of many years lay in manuscript form.

For two hours he was visibly distressed, and at one point he informed the company that the home of a certain friend, whom he named, was in ashes. Finally, at eight o'clock he exclaimed, "Thank God! The fire is extinguished, only three doors from my house!"

So compelling was the distinguished guest's narration that the story was relayed on that very evening to the provincial governor, who insisted on interviewing Swedenborg thoroughly about his "vision" of the Stockholm fire. The careful scientist provided a detailed account of how the fire started, how long it lasted, and in what manner it was finally brought under control. A messenger arrived from Stockholm three days after the alleged fire. The letters he brought with him verified Swedenborg's account to the very last detail.

When news of Swedenborg's amazing "second sight" spread throughout Sweden, it placed their dignified celebrity in quite a new light. Within eighteen months two more episodes involving famed citizens served to add fuel to the sensation, though these episodes were neither sought by

Swedenborg, nor did he try to promote them afterwards.

They both occurred in the year 1760, and the first one concerned the Queen herself. The prime minister of Sweden, Count Anders von Hopken, a witness to the event, provides the following account:

> Swedenborg was one day at a court reception. Her majesty asked him about different things in the other life, and lastly, whether he had seen or talked with her brother, the Prince Royal of Prussia [who had recently died]. He answered, No. Her Majesty then requested him to ask after him, and give him her greeting, which Swedenborg promised to do. I doubt whether the Queen meant this seriously. At the next reception, Swedenborg again appeared at court; and while the Queen was surrounded by her ladies of honour, he came boldly in and approached Her Majesty . . . Swedenborg not only greeted her from her brother, but also gave her his apologies for not having answered her last letter; he wished to do so now through Swedenborg; which he accordingly did. The Queen was greatly overcome, and said, "No one but God knows this secret."

Also that same year Madame Marteville, the widow of the Dutch ambassador to Stockholm, came to Swedenborg for a peculiar, but urgent favor. She had received a bill for an expensive silver service for which she was certain her husband had paid. She could not, however, locate the receipt anywhere, and the silversmith was demanding payment. In desperation, she finally approached Swedenborg and requested if he might ask her deceased husband about the matter.

He came to her home a few days later when Madame Marteville was entertaining guests. "I questioned your husband. He confirmed that he paid for the tea service, and he says that the receipt is in the bureau upstairs."

"Impossible," the widow answered. "I've searched it completely."

Swedenborg then explained that there was a hidden compartment behind the top left-hand drawer. The ambassador had never alerted her to it, but she would find there not only the receipt, but also other important papers. The entire company then marched upstairs to witness the outcome. The drawer was pulled all the way out and, to be sure, the hidden compartment was revealed containing exactly the contents described by Swedenborg.

THE FINAL TASK

Swedenborg himself put little stock in these episodes that so impressed many of his friends. The events had occurred naturally in the course of his life, and although they allowed his actual daily state of consciousness to become known to others, he felt he had one mission only: to reveal the true Christian religion, which had been badly distorted over the centuries by the ecclesiastical organizations.

He understood his task to be the publication of printed works that would last for generations, and he wrote steadily and faithfully, almost until the day he died at the age of eighty-four. He left behind a set of astonishing spiritual books that occupy thirty volumes in English. By his own testimony, from the time of his Christ encounter to the day of his death, he enjoyed continual access to the spiritual realm. In this highly clairvoyant and clairaudient state Swedenborg laid out a liberating new understanding of religious truth that ultimately made a deep impact on Western thought.

Throughout these books he never strays from his careful observational style that he learned as a scientist. Even when discussing the most celestial subjects, his focus is always down-to-earth. His clear intention is to help the reader see God, even when he is discussing episodes in the spiritual world that seem incredible to us. Through the sincerity of his writing, his goal is never lost: the enlightenment of people so that they may live lives that lead to heavenly states.

Theological and Spiritual Writings of Emanuel Swedenborg

THE APOCALYPSE EXPLAINED, *6 volumes*
Swedenborg's symbolic interpretation of the Book of Revelation and other parts of the Bible, particularly the Psalms, the Prophets, and the Gospels.

THE APOCALYPSE REVEALED, *2 volumes*
A study which concentrates on the spiritual symbolic sense of the Book of Revelation.

ARCANA COELESTIA [Heavenly Secrets], *12 volumes*
Swedenborg explores the spiritual sense of the allegory and history of the books of Genesis and Exodus.

CHARITY
In this volume the concept of charity is enlarged to embrace the whole range of human activity.

CONJUGIAL LOVE
An ethical discussion of the relation of the sexes and the origin and nature of marital love.

DIVINE LOVE AND WISDOM
An interpretation of the universe as a spiritual-natural, or psychophysical, world. This work describes the creation of the universe and the three discrete degrees of mind.

DIVINE PROVIDENCE
Swedenborg's philosophical work describes how God cares for the individual and for humanity.

THE FOUR DOCTRINES

Swedenborg interprets four leading doctrines of Christianity: The Lord, the Scriptures, Life and Faith.

HEAVEN AND HELL

Based on his visionary experiences, Swedenborg gives us a comprehensive account of our entry into the next world and life after death.

MISCELLANEOUS THEOLOGICAL WORKS

Bound together in this volume are the following treatises: The New Jerusalem and Its Heavenly Doctrine; A Brief Exposition of the Doctrine of the New Church; The Nature of Intercourse Between the Soul and the Body; On the White Horse Mentioned in the Apocalypse; On the Earths in the Universe; The Last Judgment; and A Continuation Concerning the Last Judgment.

POSTHUMOUS THEOLOGICAL WORKS, *2 volumes*

A collection of shorter posthumous works, including extracts from Swedenborg's personal correspondence.

THE SPIRITUAL DIARY, *5 volumes*

A storehouse of spiritual facts, phenomena and principles written by Swedenborg at the time of his experiences in the spiritual realm over a period of some twenty years.

TRUE CHRISTIAN RELIGION, *2 volumes*

Swedenborg's teachings for the New Christian Era, dealing with a broad spectrum of relevant concerns for the contemporary reader.

An Invitation to Read Heaven and Hell

by Helen Keller

I was first introduced to Emanuel Swedenborg's *Heaven and Hell* by a dear friend, Mr. John Hitz, while I was still in my teens.

When I began *Heaven and Hell*, I was as little aware of the new joy coming into my life as I had been years before when I stood on the piazza steps awaiting my teacher. Impelled only by the curiosity of a young girl who loves to read, I opened that big Braille book, and lo, my fingers lighted upon a paragraph in the preface about a blind woman whose darkness was illumined with beautiful truths from Swedenborg's writings. She believed they imparted a light to her mind which more than compensated her for the loss of earthly light. She never doubted that there was a spiritual body within the material one with perfect senses, and that after a few dark years the eyes within her eyes would open to a world infinitely more wonderful, complete, and satisfying than this.

My heart gave a joyous bound. Here was a faith that emphasized what I felt so keenly—the separateness between soul and body, between a realm I could picture as a whole and the chaos of fragmentary things and irrational contingencies which my limited physical senses met at every turn. I let myself go, as healthy, happy youth will, and tried to puzzle out the weighty thoughts of the Swedish sage. Somehow I sensed the likeness of Him whom I loved as the One and Only, and I wanted to understand more. The words Love and Wisdom seemed to caress my fingers from paragraph to paragraph, and these two words released in me new forces to stimulate my somewhat indolent nature and urge me forward evermore. As I realized the meaning of what I read, my soul seemed to expand and gain confidence amid the difficulties which beset me.

The descriptions of the other world bore me far, far over measureless regions bathed in superhuman beauty and strangeness, where angels' robes flash, where great lives and creative minds cast a splendor upon darkest circumstances, where events and mighty combats sweep by endlessly, where the night is lit to eternal day by the smile of God. I glowed through and through as I sat in that atmosphere of the soul and watched men and women of nobler mold pass in majestic procession. For the first time immortality put on intelligibility for me, the earth wore new curves of loveliness and significance. I was glad to discover that the City of God was not a stupid affair of glass streets and sapphire walls, but a systematic treasury of wise, helpful thoughts and noble influences. Gradually I came to see that I could use the Bible, which had baffled me, as an instrument for digging out precious truths, just as I could use my hindered, halting body for the high behests of my spirit.

Heaven, as Swedenborg portrays it, is not a mere collection of radiant ideas, but a practical, livable world. It should never be forgotten that death is not the end of life, but only one of its most important experiences. In the great silence of my thoughts, all those whom I have loved on earth, whether near or far, living or dead, live and have their own individuality, their own dear ways and charm. At any moment I can bring them around me to cheer my loneliness. It would break my heart if any barrier could prevent them from coming to me. But I know there are two worlds—one we can measure with line and rule, and other we can feel with our hearts and intuitions.

Swedenborg makes the future life not only conceivable, but desirable. His message to the living who meet the might of death with its attendant separation and sorrow sweeps across the heart of humanity life some sweet breath from God's Presence. We can now meet death as Nature does, in a blaze of glory, marching to the grave with a gay step, wearing our brightest thoughts and most brilliant anticipations.

As I wander through the dark, encountering difficulties, I am aware of encouraging voices that murmur from the spirit realm. I sense a holy passion pouring down from the springs of Infinity. I thrill to music that beats with the pulses of God. Bound to suns and planets by invisible cords, I feel the flame of eternity in my soul. Here in the midst of everyday air, I sense the rush of ethereal rains. I am conscious of the splendor that binds all things of earth to all things of heaven—immured by silence and darkness, I possess the light which shall give me vision a thousand-fold when death sets me free.

(These comments are excerpted from Helen Keller's book, *My Religion*, written in 1960 as a tribute to Emanuel Swedenborg.)

For a special discount on Swedenborg's *Heaven & Hell* (505 pages, paperback) send $5 (postpaid) to:

Order Department
J. Appleseed & Co.
3200 Washington St.
San Francisco, CA 94115

About the Publisher

During the first half of the 19th century, an itinerant nurseryman named John Chapman criss-crossed thousands of miles planting apple orchards from the Ohio River to the Great Lakes. His unique worldly activity together with a singularly spiritual personality gave genesis to the legends of Johnny Appleseed. The spiritual inspiration for his life's work came to him through his less well-known cargo: the writings of Emanuel Swedenborg. Along with his apple seeds, he deposited Swedenborg books throughout the Midwest for forty years. Sometimes, when his inventory ran low, Johnny would tear a book in half, leaving one part with one farmer and the other with another, and then switch them when he came back through. Nothing gave him greater satisfaction than to discuss and share his "Good News, fresh from Heaven!" Today, we seek to expand the spiritual orchard that Johnny began.

J. Appleseed & Co.

3200 Washington Street

San Francisco, CA 94115

Information on Swedenborg and Swedenborgian Literature

In the United States

Swedenborg Foundation
P.O. Box 549
West Chester, PA 19381-0549
1-800-355-3222

In Canada

Information Swedenborg
4939 B Dundas Street W.
Etobicoke, Ontario M9A 1B6